Carolyn Slaughter

FOLLOWING JESUS

steps to a passionate faith

Leader Guide

ABINGDON PRESS
NASHVILLE

FOLLOWING JESUS:
STEPS TO A PASSIONATE FAITH—LEADER GUIDE

Copyright © 2008 by Abingdon Press

All rights reserved.

This book is printed on acid-free paper.

ISBN 978-0-687-64948-8

08 09 10 11 12 13 14 15 16 17 – 10 9 8 7 6 5 4 3 2 1
MANUFACTURED IN THE UNITED STATES OF AMERICA

TABLE OF CONTENTS

INTRODUCTION

I serve on the Adult Education staff team at Ginghamsburg United Methodist Church in Tipp City, Ohio. The content you will discover in the pages of this curriculum has been used (in many different forms) over the past three decades to systematically train followers of Jesus at Ginghamsburg for a life of radical discipleship and service. This course serves as the membership class at Ginghamsburg, preparing potential members to fully live out God's call on their lives. Regardless of their intention towards membership, everyone is encouraged to complete this class as a means of exploring the Christian faith and what it means to follow Jesus.

With *Following Jesus: Steps to a Passionate Faith*, the membership curriculum we use at Ginghamsburg Church is now available to a wider church audience. You'll find that the sessions in *Following Jesus* contain many activities and are very full. In order to make sure that relationship building occurs (definitely a primary goal of the class), it may be necessary to revise or combine some activities to fit your class and setting. While we want you to benefit from the activities we've tested, I trust you, as a wise and experienced leader, to listen to the Lord as the session progresses. Make the sessions benefit the students! The curriculum is simply a guide.

How to Use This Book

This book is designed to help you lead others through a basic study of the Christian faith. *Following Jesus: Steps to a Passionate Faith* includes twelve sessions and covers three major areas of study: Rediscovering Jesus, Growing in the Spirit, and Living in Faith and Service. As background on what it means to be a follower of Jesus, you may want to encourage your class members to read *Spiritual Entrepreneurs* (Abingdon, 1995) or *Real Followers* (Abingdon, 1999), both by Michael Slaughter, as you proceed through this study. Discussion questions from *Spiritual Entrepreneurs* are included in Sessions Four, Five, Six, Ten, Eleven, and Twelve. Additional background material and links to useful resources are available to you at http://ginghamsburg.org/followingjesus.

In addition to the regular sessions, we encourage you to organize for your participants at least two fellowship events outside the regular class setting. This will help assimilate newcomers into the community life of your church. One of these fellowship events should include your senior pastor, allowing your participants to personally meet your pastor and to ask any questions they may have about the church or the Christian faith.

To use this curriculum as the basis of a membership class, I suggest:
• Clearly define with each class what membership means at your particular local church.
• Establish attendance standards for those who are fulfilling the membership process. At Ginghamsburg Church, we require students to attend 75% of the classes (three allowed absences) with make-up work required for the missed classes.

- Be clear in setting expectations for your members. We ask our members to commit to four life practices that will keep them growing as body life members in Christ's church as well as investing in Christ's mission as expressed through the local church:
  - Faithful participation in weekly worship celebrations
  - Faithful participation in a small group for growth and accountability
  - Faithful use of their spiritual gifts and talents in service to others
  - Faithful support of the church through their tithe and financial gifts
- Provide a one-on-one conference at the end of the class for each participant to talk to a church leader and complete his or her entry into a ministry area. The membership interview form we use at Ginghamsburg Church is included in Session Ten as an example of a document to use as the basis of this conference.
- Encourage each person to prayerfully and thoughtfully consider his or her willingness and ability to commit to membership at the end of the twelve class sessions. There is no pressure to make that commitment until the person is ready—even if that time is significantly in the future.
- With each class, provide an opportunity for persons to be baptized or have their baptisms reaffirmed prior to membership weekend.

A Note About Leaders

Class leaders are critical, not only to the quality and success of this course, but also to the relationship of participants with the church. Class leaders are often among the first points of church contact for the participants. Therefore, the leaders must have a deep and seasoned walk with Christ as well as a firm grasp of Christianity and your local congregation.

We encourage co-leadership based on the principles of discipleship and the example of Jesus sending out disciples in groups of two.

Leadership could consist of co-leaders or a leader and an apprentice (someone who is being discipled to teach). Alongside the teachers, at Ginghamsburg we staff each class with a group of table facilitators that we call "networkers." Their purpose is exactly what the name implies: to network with class members around the tables during class discussions and to help the class members network with opportunities for service or fellowship within the church. They are the care team and point of connection for class members during the twelve weeks of class.

The team of leaders must consist of individuals who:
• believe that God has called them to this ministry;
• have spiritual gifts in the areas of teaching, service, and/or exhortation;
• are good communicators;
• have the quality of life appropriate for a Christian leader or role model;
• are sensitive to people;
• are willing and able to spend the necessary time in study and prayer to fully prepare for each class.

I experience God and individuals in new and touching ways each time I teach this curriculum. God's Word truly is alive and consistently applicable in every new situation. May God bless you as you lead the people of your congregation through these steps in developing their passionate faith.

Carolyn Slaughter

Part 1
Rediscovering Jesus

1

SESSION ONE

JESUS THE MESSIAH

Prepare for the Session

Supplies Needed
- chalkboard or dry-erase board and markers
- Bibles
- participant books and copies of the "Who Are You?" handout
- pens/pencils

Before class, read Session One from the participant book. Imagine how participants may be feeling about what they are reading. Consider the questions they may bring with them to the class session.

Group Discussion - Who Are You?

Have participants form groups of four to six. If you have a group of six or fewer, work together in a single group. Provide each person with a writing utensil and the "Who Are You?" handout (p. 19). Allow a few minutes for everyone to complete the handout, then give each group five minutes to get to know one another in their small groups. Have each group merge with another group, so you have groups of eight to twelve participants. Ask participants to take turns introducing each other to the larger group they have just joined. When everyone has finished, gather participants and collect the handouts.

Purpose of the Study

Open the session with prayer. **Begin this first session by explaining the purpose of the study and what will be expected of the participants.** *Following Jesus: Steps to a Passionate Faith* is designed to give an overview of Christianity and what it means to follow Jesus. Since this course is foundational to understanding a personal relationship with Christ and discipleship, it is important for students to make a commitment to attend and fully participate in all the classes. If for some reason one or more participants cannot attend all the sessions, help them work out a way to participate fully.

Who Is Jesus?

Ask participants to call out descriptions of how various people describe Jesus. Write their answers on a chalkboard or dry-erase board. Then ask:
- *How do most people come to conclusions about Jesus like these?* (hearsay, tradition, opinion, own study)
- *How do they know whether or not they are right?* Pull out one of the "Who Are You?" handouts from the previous activity. Pass around the handout and ask various people to tell the class

something about that person based upon what is written on the handout. After a minute or so, thank the person and ask:

- *How is this different from how the conclusions we listed about Jesus are determined?* (came from an authoritative source, can be corroborated by other sources, is personally gathered information rather than hearsay)

Origin of the Bible

Discuss the history of the Bible and why Christians believe that it is the Word of God. The Bible is a Christian's fact base—the basis of faith and life practices. As we learn in 2 Timothy 3:16, the Bible is God-breathed, the very words of God whispered into the ears and hearts of its human writers. It is God's tool used to transform and equip us to do God's work.

The word *bible* comes from the Greek *ta biblia*, meaning "the scrolls" or "the books." Although today we think of the Bible as a single work, it is actually a group of books written by a variety of authors. They were first written on individual scrolls of paper, but around 450 B.C. the documents were edited and compiled into what we now call the Old Testament.

> "All scripture is inspired by God and is useful for teaching, for reproof, for correction, and for training in righteousness, so that everyone who belongs to God may be proficient, equipped for every good work." (2 Timothy 3:16-17, NRSV)

Following Jesus' death and resurrection, various witnesses (or disciples of eyewitnesses) recorded the life of Jesus and the early church. Included in these writings were also letters of instructions to new churches across the Middle East. Together, these writings are what we call the New Testament. The list of books to be included in the New Testament was finalized in A.D. 376 and is the New Testament we know today.

The Bible is God's means of communication with us in written form. It consists of 66 books, but one story is told through the entire Bible. It is the love story of a personal, holy God who created human beings to be in relationship with God. When that relationship was

The Gutenberg Bible was the first book to be printed in quantity with movable metal type. Johannes Gutenberg spent about three years, from 1452 to 1455, to produce about 180 copies of this Bible.

Today the Bible is the best-selling and most widely distributed book in the world, with six billion copies sold in more than 2,000 languages and dialects.

broken, this loving God pursued humans and put together a plan to restore their broken relationship.

Written over a 1,600-year period by approximately 50 different human authors, one consistent theme flows through the entire text from Genesis to Revelation: what God was willing to do to be in relationship with us.

Although consisting of one story, the Bible is divided into two sections. The Old Testament is made up of the first 39 books and covers the ancient time period from Creation to around 50 B.C. The Old Testament time is known as B.C. (before Christ). After Jesus Christ came to earth, time was reordered and is now dated as A.D. (*anno Domini*, "in the year of our Lord"). The New Testament covers the time from Jesus' birth to approximately A.D. 100. In today's session, we will focus on insights about Jesus from the Old Testament.

The Prophecy of the Coming Messiah

In Isaiah 48:3-6, God told the purpose of the Old Testament messianic prophecies (references to the person God would send to free people and bring them into a personal relationship with God):

I foretold the former things long ago, my mouth announced them and I made them known; then suddenly I acted, and they came to pass. For I knew how stubborn you were; the sinews of your neck were iron, your forehead was bronze. Therefore I told you these things long ago; before they happened I announced them to you so that you could not say, "My images brought them about; my wooden image and metal god ordained them." You have heard these things; look at them all. Will you not admit them?

God knows how stubborn humans are and how, left to our own devices, we will come up with our own reasons for whatever happens.

But God wanted the people to know who was in control of all that was being done. No credit was to go to false gods of wood and bronze. Reading Scripture from the Old Testament foretelling of the purpose of the coming Messiah and seeing that purpose and promise fulfilled in Jesus reveals to us God's plan for humankind.

Group Discussion - Messianic Prophecies

The fulfillment of specific prophecies is an important part of identifying Jesus as the Messiah. Form six groups and point each group to the list of prophecies on pages 12–13 of the participant book. It's okay if a "group" is just one person. We will use this representative sample of prophecies and see what the prophecies tell us about who Jesus is. The same set of verses is provided below. The first Bible verse is the Old Testament prophecy, and the second verse is the New Testament fulfillment of that prophecy. Assign each group one of the Scripture sets.

In their groups, have participants discuss the Scriptures assigned to them. Have them write down their observations and be prepared to share their findings with the rest of the class. Information on each set of verses is given below to support you in the class discussion.

A. Isaiah 7:14; Matthew 1:18-25—The first clue God gave to identify the Messiah was that a virgin would have a child who was fathered by the Holy Spirit. It is important to understand the significance of the virgin birth. God set up the sacrificial system in the Old Testament to provide a means of forgiveness for God's people. Animal sacrifices were made on behalf of people, with the blood of the sacrificed animal satisfying God's judgment for human sin. Only a perfect, unblemished animal qualified to be the sacrifice. Because of humans' cycle of sin, this ritual had to be observed repeatedly. In the New Testament we see that ultimately God offered Jesus, God's Son, as the final sacrifice for our sins. On the basis of the virgin birth, Jesus was fully human (the son of a human mother) and also fully divine (the

Son of God). Jesus had to be like us in human form in order to stand in our place, but he had to be without blemish or sin to provide the sacrifice God required. Only the perfect Son of God could be an adequate sacrifice to remove our sin and reconnect us with God the Father.

B. Micah 5:2; Luke 2:1-7—The Messiah would be born in Bethlehem. This prophecy described a specific place where God (who is before all things and has always existed from eternity) would enter time and space. From the Christmas story in Luke we know Jesus was born in Bethlehem.

C. Isaiah 40:3; Matthew 3:1-3 and 11:7-11—The Messiah would be preceded by a messenger—John the Baptist—who would prepare people for the Messiah's ministry.

D. Isaiah 35:3-6; Matthew 9:27-35 and 11:1-6—The Messiah would be a miracle worker and have a ministry of healing. The eyes and ears of people would be opened, both physically and spiritually. Jesus, in Matthew 9 and 11, is described as healing the blind, the lame, and curing every disease.

E. Zechariah 9:9; Luke 19:28-36—Zechariah is very specific in describing the Messiah's entrance into Jerusalem on the back of a donkey. This illustrates how specific God's prophecies were, which made the chance of all prophecies being fulfilled in one person a very low probability. And, according to Luke, Jesus entered Jerusalem the Sunday before his crucifixion in just that way.

F. Isaiah 53:4-6, 11-12; Luke 23:32-34; 2 Corinthians 5:18-21—The Messiah would bear the sins of many and intercede for those separated from God. Jesus, on the cross, fulfilled the sacrifice for our sins yesterday, today, and forever. Even though he had the sinless, divine nature of God, Jesus voluntarily took on the payment for our sins; and in the midst of the process he interceded for the world. According to Hebrews 7:23-25, Jesus is still prayerfully interceding for us today.

These are only a few of the hundreds of prophecies of the Christ found in the Old Testament, but they give us an understanding of God's perfect plan. Through the prophecies, God was saying to the world, "This is how you identify my plan. When all of these signs come together, that is my person—the Messiah, the savior of the world." All of the prophecies did come together in Jesus, and they help us begin to understand the amazing truth about who Jesus is.

New Testament Use of Prophecies

People all through the New Testament pointed to the fulfillment of prophecy as one way to authenticate who Jesus is. Share with the class a brief background on the persons speaking in the verses listed below; then read what Paul, Philip, and Jesus himself had to say about the importance of fulfilled prophecy.

- *John 1:43-45.* Philip was one of the first of Jesus' disciples; and he called others to join him in following "the one Moses wrote about in the Law, and about whom the prophets also wrote—Jesus of Nazareth, son of Joseph" (1:45).
- *Luke 24:44-48.* Jesus himself pointed to the Old Testament and said, "Everything must be fulfilled that is written about me in the Law of Moses, the Prophets and the Psalms" (24:44).
- *Acts 17:1-4.* Paul, a Pharisee and persecutor of the early church who was converted on the road to Damascus, became one of the great defenders of the faith. He pointed to fulfilled prophecy as he taught about Jesus in the Jewish synagogues.

Reflection - Who Do You Say That I Am?

The question *Who is Jesus?* is one that everyone must answer at some point in his or her life. Jesus asked his own disciples that very question while he was still on earth in human form. The incident is recorded in Matthew 16:13-16. Ask a participant to read the passage out loud. Afterward, ask each person to ask themselves, based on what they know about Jesus so far, who Jesus is to them. Have them write the answer to the question in their participant books.

Group Discussion

Have participants form pairs and tell each other one or two ways in which their lives have changed or they hope their lives will change as a result of learning the truth about who Jesus is. When pairs are finished, close the class in prayer.

Closing Prayer

Lord, I praise you for sending Jesus, the Messiah, to reconnect us with God forever and to serve as the ultimate example for the way we should live our lives. Thank you, God, for giving us your love story for humanity in written form. Please open my heart to a deeper walk with Jesus and empower me to live more fully for Jesus this week.

Homework

Before dismissing the group, remind participants to prepare for next week. The assignment is to browse through the first four books of the New Testament—Matthew, Mark, Luke, and John. These are the books that primarily tell the story of Jesus. Also, ask class members to read and complete Session Two in the participant book.

Who Are You?

Name:

_____

Address:

_____

City: _____ State:_____ ZIP code: _____

Phone: _____ Cell Phone: _____

Email: _____ Birthday: _____

Occupation: _____ Marital Status: _____

Children's Names and Ages:

_____

_____

What do you do for fun?

_____

_____

What is special about you that you want people to know?

_____

_____

How long have you attended this church?

_____

_____

What do you hope to gain from this class?

_____

_____

How would you describe what it means to be a Christian?

_____

_____

How would you describe your faith experience up to this point in your life?

_____

_____

2

SESSION TWO
THE UNIQUENESS OF JESUS

Prepare for the Session

Supplies Needed
- chalkboard or dry-erase board and markers
- Bibles
- participant books
- pens/pencils

After an opening prayer and welcome, share with the group that in this session we will look more deeply at the identity of Jesus through what his contemporaries said about him and what Jesus himself had to say about who he is. Through our study of Scripture, we will also discover some of the unique characteristics of Jesus. We are looking at all of this in the context of Matthew 16:15, when Jesus asked his followers, "Who do you say I am?"

Ice Breaker

Have participants divide into groups of three or four. Then ask them to discuss:
- What would your contemporaries say is unique about you as a person?
- In what way do you think you are unique? (This could be a personal quality, a career position, a relationship, etc.)

Allow about five minutes of discussion, then have each group share a couple of ideas with the larger group.

What Makes Jesus Unique?

Assign one of the Scriptures from the list below to each of your small groups (or to pairs or individuals in smaller classes) to look up and read through (Scripture list also appears in the participant book, p. 18). It's okay if more than one group or individual is assigned the same Scripture or more than one set of Scriptures is assigned to the same group or individual. From their verses they are to answer this question: *Based on these Scriptures, how is Jesus unique?* When individuals or groups have read their assigned Scriptures, have them report to the larger group the unique quality they found that sets Jesus apart from all others. Ideas are included to help you guide the class discussion. Ask the group, "What have you learned about Jesus and who he is?"

- Matthew 1:18-25—*Jesus had a unique birth and genealogy.*
- John 8:28-30; 1 Peter 1:18-19; Luke 23:39-43—*Jesus is sinless.*
- Matthew 8:23-27; John 2:1-11—*Jesus performs miracles.*
- John 20:1-18; Matthew 9:23-26—*Jesus has power over death.*
- Luke 7:40-50; Acts 10:39-43; Matthew 9:1-8—*Jesus has authority to forgive us and cleanse us from our sins.*
- John 6:28-35; 4:9-15—*Jesus satisfies spiritual hunger and thirst.*

Each of us has qualities that make us unique, but the more we learn about Jesus the more we see that his unique qualities set him apart from every other person who has ever lived. Now we'll explore more of the unique things that Jesus' contemporaries said about him as well as the unique things he said about himself.

Group Work and Discussion

Divide participants into two groups. Have the groups refer to pages 18–20 in their participant books. Using the first list of Scriptures and their Bibles, have one group discuss the question: *What did Jesus say about himself?* Have the other group do the same with the second list of Scriptures for the question: *What did Jesus' contemporaries say about him?* Say, "These Scriptures reveal more about Jesus. As you read these Scriptures, ask who, what, when, where, and how questions for each verse. Read not just to discover a point but also to understand what the passage says to you."

He Said, They Said

What Did Jesus Say About Himself?

Have the group focusing on the Scriptures from John share what they discovered about Jesus' identity and his purpose from these texts. Precede the group reports by sharing with the group that in the Gospel of John, Jesus made many statements beginning with "I am" that helped his followers understand his identity and purpose. These include some memorable phrases like "I am the bread of life," "I am the light of the world," "I am the good shepherd," and "I am the way, the truth, and the life." Here are some helps to guide the discussion if needed:

John 4:21-26
- "I am he"—Jesus identifies himself as the Messiah to the woman at the well. This is his first declaration of his identity as

Messiah and he did so to a disenfranchised person: a woman (the discounted gender) who was also a Samaritan (a victim of racial discrimination).

John 8:12
- The "light of the world" shining God's love into darkness
- Draws persons to the light

John 10:7-15
- "The gate"—Jesus serves as the gate to a personal relationship with God and provides for the sheep within the fold.
- "Good shepherd"—Jesus is the protector who lays down his life for the sheep.

John 13:6-17
- "Teacher and Lord"
- One who leads by example
- Absolute authority
- Ultimate servant
- A different kind of God

John 14:5-10
- "The way and the truth and the life"
- The only path to God
- The reality of all God's promises; the truth about God
- The source of life and the power to live a godly life

John 15:1-8
- The "vine"—the source of everything you need to follow Jesus fully
- Jesus produces fruit through his followers
- The source of discipleship through connection and obedience to him

John 17:1-5
- The Son of God
- The source of eternal life
- Existed before time, active in creation (see Genesis 1:26)

What Did Jesus' Contemporaries Say About Him?

We have heard what Jesus told his followers about himself. Let's look at what Jesus' early followers said about him. Many of these followers were the closest persons to Jesus, living and traveling with him in good times and bad. Jesus revealed his identity to them through teachings and stories, miracles and prayers; some recognized Jesus for who he was immediately, while others grew into that understanding over time. **Ask the group focusing on these Scriptures to share what they discovered about Jesus' identity and his purpose from these texts. Here are some summaries to help with discussion:**

John (John 1:1-14)—John was one of the inner core of three disciples along with his brother, James, and Peter. John was considered to be Jesus' closest friend and was present on all major occasions with him. John wrote the Gospel of John, three letters found at the end of the New Testament, and the Book of Revelation.
- *"Logos"* (verse 1)—the "Word" understood by both Greek and Jew as the power controlling the universe. John's word for God.
- God in the flesh (verses 1-3)
- Creator (verse 3)
- The source of two kinds of life: physically through our creation and spiritually through our redemption (verses 4-5)
- The Light revealing life to world (verse 9)
- Many choose not to receive and know God through Jesus (verses 10-11)

25

- But those who put their faith in him are established as children in the family of God (verse 12)
- God took on human form and was revealed to us in the flesh (verse 14)
- He possessed all attributes of divinity and humanity except sin
- Created the new covenant with humankind by dying in our place
- His divine nature qualified him as payment for sin (unblemished sacrifice)

Peter (Matthew 16:16)—Peter also was one of the inner circle of three disciples and was also present on all major occasions with Jesus. Peter ran a fishing business and had a brash and bold personality. He is the symbol for redemption after abject failure in following Jesus.
- The Christ, the Son of the Living God
- Christ equals *Messiah*—the one they were expecting

Martha (John 11:27)—Martha was part of a family who lived in Bethany and was close to Jesus. Her siblings were Lazarus (whom Jesus raised from the dead) and Mary. This family frequently hosted Jesus in their home.
- The Christ
- The Son of God
- The One (God) who has come into the world

Stephen (Acts 7:59)—Stephen was not one of the original twelve disciples but was an early convert and leader in the Jerusalem church. He was known for his serving and administrative gifts. Stephen was the first martyr for Christ.
- "Lord Jesus, receive my spirit"
- He recognized Jesus as God—the one who has authority over souls

Thomas (John 20:26-29)—Thomas has the dubious honor of being known as the "Doubter." One of the original twelve disciples, Thomas was not present for Jesus' post-resurrection appearance to the disciples and expressed doubt at what the other disciples had seen. He demonstrates the care God gives each individual and how gently God deals with our doubts.

- My Lord and my God

Paul (Colossians 1:15-20)—Paul was a persistent persecutor of the newly established church in the first century. Trained as a Pharisee and expert on the Old Testament Law, Paul had a dramatic conversion experience on the road to Damascus. His total turn-around found him using his training in the Law to reason with people in order to win them to Christ. He wrote much of the New Testament.

- The One who is the visible image of our invisible God
- The Resurrection, the hope of life
- The fullness of God
- The source of our reconciliation with God.
- The one who holds all things together

After each group or individual reports back to the class, ask the class: "How can we be confident that Jesus' contemporaries weren't fabricating stories about Jesus or lying about what they really knew about him?"

The following Scriptures record what two of Jesus' followers had to say about this question. Ask a participant to read Luke 1:1-4 and 1 John 1:1-3.

Luke was a physician. We learn from his writings that Luke possessed a scientific mind and was interested in knowing and communicating the facts. He was not a person who let his imagination roam when writing about Jesus. Luke was a close friend and traveling companion of Paul. He was an eyewitness to the birth and growth of the early church and had access to the other disciples for information gathering. Luke took these eyewitness accounts and put them in organized form.

In the same way, John's Gospel and Letters are based on eyewitness accounts to the events of Jesus' life. In 1 John 1:1, John says, "That which was from the beginning, which we have heard, which we have seen with our eyes, which we have looked at and our hands have touched—this we proclaim concerning the Word of Life" (NIV).

These independent reports agree on who Jesus was and what he did.

Responding to Jesus

Because our goal in our Christian life is to be transformed, not merely informed, we must do something with the information we have been gathering. As we consider the question from Matthew 16, "Who do you say I am?" we must begin narrowing the responses and make an individual decision concerning Jesus. In John's Gospel, Jesus equates himself with God; and the testimonies of others agree. Now, each of us must choose to agree or disagree with them.

Reflection

Have participants refer to their answers to the questions on page 21 of the participant book. Have the participants form pairs; then ask them to discuss these questions:

- Based on what you now know about Jesus, do you think he really is who he claims to be? Explain.
- What qualities or claims of Jesus do you find appealing?
- What qualities or claims of Jesus challenge you?
- If Jesus were physically in the room, would you like to meet him personally and spend time getting to know him? Why or why not?

Closing Prayer

I ask, God, for you to open my eyes and heart to your Word and the reality of who Jesus is. I pray that Jesus will become even more real to me and that he will reveal himself to me in even greater ways. Empower me this week to serve others and be all I can be for you.

Homework

Ask the class to read and complete Session Three in the participant book.

3

SESSION THREE
SAVIOR OF THE WORLD

Prepare for the Session

Supplies Needed
- chalkboard or dry-erase board and markers
- Bibles
- participant books
- pens/pencils
- small, wrapped gifts (can be as small as a piece of candy)

Additional helps: If your church has a handout on becoming a Christian, it might be helpful to have these for any participants who want more information and support. Christian organizations such as Intervarsity Christian Fellowship, The Navigators, Campus Crusade for Christ, and the Billy Graham Evangelistic Association have materials that you can order.

As class members arrive for this session, give each person a small, wrapped gift, and tell them it's a little gift from you.

Ice Breaker

After opening the class with welcome and prayer, have small groups look at one or both of these excerpts from Michael Slaughter's book, *Spiritual Entrepreneurs* (Abingdon Press, 1995), and discuss the questions that follow:

I have visited many Sunday school classes when the people were...studying the lives of Abraham, Moses, David, or one of the other biblical characters. Information is given about 4,000-year-old people, and we feel that the purpose of the class has been accomplished. Scripture was not given for information. It was given that we might see the One who is the author of life and be radically transformed through him. (p. 53)

Renewal happens as the church moves from a vague theism to a clear faith in Jesus Christ. The focus of the church is not church, but Jesus! God is made known to us in Christ. Faith comes alive in Christ. Lives are transformed and empowered through Christ. (p. 32)

- What does it mean to be radically transformed?
- How do you see transformation in lives of Christian people or through the church?
- How do you see transformation happening in your own life?

After allowing time for group discussion, have one person from each group report to the larger group the highlights of what they discussed.

Why Did Jesus Come?

In today's session we will focus on the source of life transformation: a personal relationship with Jesus. We will work through a short Bible study looking for the answers to the question, *Why did*

Jesus come? In small groups, help the class work through the Scriptures listed in the participant books and reflect on the questions related to each set of passages. This study is divided into three sections. After the groups complete each section, bring the groups together to pool insights and make sure they understand the point of each Scripture. Information is provided for you after each section to include in the class discussion.

The Sin Problem

The Scriptures in this first section help us understand the human problem of sin or separation from God. Read the following verses and answer the question:

- What have we humans done to create our own problems?
  - *Isaiah 53:6*
  - *Romans 3:9-12*
  - *Romans 3:23*
  - *John 3:19*

According to Isaiah 53:6; Romans 3:10, 23; and John 3:19, all of us are lost! We have missed the mark in fulfilling God's design for us. Humans were not created to be separated from God. God, out of great love, created us to be in perfect relationship with God. But, because of a choice made by our spiritual ancestors as told in Genesis 3, we have inherited a rebellious nature that drives us to choose anything but God. While humans were created to be in close relationship with God, the DNA of sin we carry has created a gulf between God and us, and we live with a sense of loss and disconnection from our Creator.

The following Scriptures help us understand the consequences we experience when we choose to live apart from God. Read the following verses and answer the question:

- What are the consequences of our actions?
  - *Isaiah 59:2*
  - *Romans 6:23*
  - *Romans 14:10-12*

As a result of our sinful nature, we live out of sync with God and show symptoms of being lost through such things as addictive behaviors; shallow relationships; a sense of not being fulfilled; and the lack of peace, power, and purpose. Romans 6:23 tells us sin brings death to hope, relationships, and accomplishing God's design for our lives. Left uncorrected, sin brings spiritual death that separates us from God for eternity. Romans 14 warns that we will have to give an account of our lives to God. God's law of restitution, just like our justice system in the United States, requires by law that restitution be made when a party is offended—a penalty enforced and possibly fines paid. According to this Scripture the penalty we earn for ongoing sin is death, or eternal separation from God. However, as we read in John 3:16-17, God offers help, hope, and a way back to wholeness with our Creator through Jesus, who paid the penalty of sin for us.

> "For God so loved the world that he gave his only Son, so that everyone who believes in him may not perish but may have eternal life. Indeed, God did not send the Son into the world to condemn the world, but in order that the world might be saved through him." (John 3:16-17, NRSV)

We have all missed the mark in fulfilling God's design for us. There is no one exempt from the influence of our fallen nature. Likewise, there is no one exempt from the great love of God.

Have groups discuss their answers to the remaining two questions on page 25 of the participant book:

- How do you, in your own life, see actions or attitudes that separate you from God?
- What one specific activity, fear, or habit do you see as the most critical in keeping you from becoming all God would hope for you?

The Jesus Remedy

We've talked about our human condition of sin and the gulf that sin creates between us and the God who created us. Let's read now to understand how Jesus changes the equation. Again have small groups address this question through study of the following Scriptures:

- How did Jesus' coming help us?
  - ○ *Isaiah 53:4-5*
  - ○ *Romans 5:8-9*
  - ○ *Titus 3:3-7*
  - ○ *Ephesians 2:8-9*

In the Old Testament, God provided forgiveness and the chance to reconnect with God through the sacrificial system. Through the sacrificial death of a perfect, unblemished animal in the place of a human, restitution was made—at least until the next sinful, rebellious act. Jesus, in the New Testament, came to be the ultimate sacrifice for our sins once and for all. Fully human to identify with us and take our place, yet fully divine (sinless) to be an acceptable sacrifice to God, Jesus made full restitution through his death. And the wonderful news is Jesus died for us while we were still sinners! We don't have to clean up our act or be "good enough" to come to God through Jesus.

Listen to the good news and the answer to our sin problem: Romans 5:8-9, "But God demonstrates his own love for us in this: While we were still sinners, Christ died for us. Since we have now been justified by his blood, how much more shall we be saved from God's wrath through him!" (NIV).

That's called grace—the totally undeserved, unearned, no-strings-attached, free gift of God.

Have groups discuss their answers to the questions about grace on page 26 of the participant book.

Repentance and Forgiveness

We know that Jesus came to offer hope, salvation, and a way back to relationship with God. That way back comes through repenting or turning away from our sins, believing and welcoming Jesus into our lives and then fully experiencing forgiveness. Let's read more from Scripture on how that happens. The next question for participants to discuss in their small groups is:

- What is our part in entering into a personal relationship with Christ and experiencing salvation? Use the following verses to identify steps we must take:
  - ❍ *Isaiah 55:7* (repent)
  - ❍ *1 John 1:8-9* (confess and accept God's forgiveness)
  - ❍ *Acts 16:31* (believe)
  - ❍ *John 1:12* (receive)

What must we do to receive salvation in Jesus and enter into a personal relationship with him? The first step is to confess our sin and agree with God that we have been choosing to live life our way, not God's way. Next, we add to confession our repentance, which is a change in heart and a purposeful turning toward God. We turn around 180 degrees to be heading away from sin and to God. The next step is to believe. The New Testament word that we translate *believe* has the actual meaning "to lean your whole weight upon." In other words, this is an active word, so much more than just an intellectual concept. It is a lifestyle of movement toward and dependence on God. We receive Christ into our hearts by faith. Jesus comes into our lives just as a guest comes into our home when we open the door; only Jesus comes for a lifelong stay—sleeping bag and all! He only needs to be invited.

Now let's look at the next question, finding our answers from Scripture once again:
- What does salvation in Jesus mean to us?
  - ❍ *Romans 4:23–5:2* (justified)
  - ❍ *Romans 8:1-2* (removed from judgment)
  - ❍ *2 Corinthians 5:17* (new start, new chances)
  - ❍ *John 5:24* (eternal life; crossed over from death to life)

To be justified means to be made clean, or "just-as-if-I'd" never sinned. Salvation means I am at peace with God—all the guilt of past failures has been removed. Because Jesus paid the price for us we are removed from judgment, we move from eternal separation from God to an eternity living in God's presence. We have a new life and brand new start in life. The original Greek language used in the New Testament includes a verb tense we don't have in English that gives rich meaning to God's intent for us. In the Greek, 2 Corinthians 5:17 says, "The old has gone and is continuing to go; the new has come and is continuing to come." We are in process in Jesus, being made new and whole every day as we practice repentance, confession, and depending on God. There is never a lack of fresh starts with Jesus.

What Does It Mean to Be a Christian?

It may take a lifetime to know how to live your Christian life; but what does it mean, in simple terms, to *be* a Christian? A Christian is someone who has repented of his or her sinful independence from God; surrendered control to Jesus; received the gift of eternal life; and made a faith commitment to follow Jesus for the rest of his or her life. A Christian's life is grounded in walking with Jesus daily. We are multi-dimensional people and we respond to a relationship with Christ and our relationships with others on different levels. We use our intellect, our emotions, and our will.

We talked at the very beginning of this session about what it means to be "radically transformed" in Christ. Being a Christian is the commitment of our whole being to Jesus Christ—all that we know of ourselves to all that we know of Jesus—so Jesus has the freedom to do his transforming work in us.

Write on the board, a flip chart, or projector: Intellect, Emotions, and Will. Ask the group what part each of these aspects of personality play in following Jesus. Ask the group (together or in small groups or pairs) to respond to what it would mean to bring your entire self, on all three of these levels, to your Christian faith?

Here is some additional help if needed as you lead the discussion:

Intellect

Christianity is based in fact; it is not a blind leap of faith. The Gospel writers carefully wrote down the historical record of Jesus' life. Christianity, including the Resurrection, is historical and can be checked out. We are free to investigate everything about our faith, but we must choose to commit to Jesus with our minds. Committing to Jesus does not mean we will never have questions or doubts. It does mean you trust what you know of Jesus and are willing to walk the uncertainties of life with him.

Emotions (passion)

As Christians we enter into a love relationship with the Lord. It is similar to a healthy marriage. In a marriage, the couple develops a bond, an attachment that continuously matures with the couple's commitment. That bond expresses itself in feelings and also in loving actions toward each other. There may be up and down times emotionally in your relationship with Christ, just like in a marriage; but what you are feeling is not the basis of your relationship or that relationship would be unstable. Instead of relying on feelings we must respond through our actions, demonstrating our love for Jesus. We must love as God first loved us.

Benefits of Following Jesus

Have students volunteer to read aloud the following passages and identify each benefit we receive through being in relationship with Christ (see participant book, p. 28).

- 2 Corinthians 5:17—We are given a new start in life. Our old ways are forgiven and forgotten. We are made new every day as we live in submission to Jesus.

- John 3:16—We are given eternal life with God.

- Romans 8:9—The Holy Spirit becomes a resident in our lives. We have the ongoing presence of Jesus with us 24/7.

- Galatians 5:22-23—Christ's character begins to form in us and continues forming each day, transforming our character into his.

- Philippians 4:19—All God's resources are at our disposal. God meets our every need.

Will

When we make a commitment to follow Jesus, it is an act of our will, a choice. It is a decision based on the reality of Jesus and faith in him. To not choose is to choose a life apart from Christ. Living out that commitment is a continuing series of choices and act of will. If we depend on our emotions and feelings to maintain our relationship, it will falter. Regardless of who we feel we are at the moment, we choose to live out of the commitment of our will. Once we invite Jesus into our lives, he has promised that he will never leave us or forsake us.

Benefits of Following Jesus

Lead the class through the exercises in the box on the previous page. Then share:

Knowing Jesus is an exciting thing! We are given a new start in life, initially when we ask Jesus into our lives, and every day as we turn our lives over to him and recommit to him once again. We are given eternal life, the promise of being in the presence of God through eternity. We are given the Holy Spirit who literally takes up residence in our lives and is the ongoing presence of Jesus within us. We are given Christ's transforming power, which is the force creating radical transformation within us and will, over a lifetime, make us over into his image. We are given all the resources of God the Father to live this life of faith.

Reflection - Time of Commitment

Say to the class: "We have spent the last weeks investigating who Jesus is and the significance of that truth for our lives. Now it's time to prayerfully consider all we've studied so far. Remember that little gift I gave you at the beginning of class? It was small, but for you to have it you had to accept it from me. The same is true of a relationship with Jesus. For you to truly have a relationship with Christ, you must accept this gift from God, open it up, and use it. If you believe that the Bible's message about Jesus is true, it's time for you to accept that message and make this commitment to Jesus. Let's pray together right now. If you are making a faith commitment to Jesus, let your study leader or your pastor know."

Closing Prayer

Thank you, Jesus, for what you did on the cross for me, for the restitution made on my behalf, and the price fully paid for my sin. I confess that I have been less than what you had in mind for me and have chosen to live life my own way and in my own efforts. Please forgive me and make me new. Thank you, Jesus, for the changes you will bring about in my life and for loving me so deeply.

Homework

Ask the class to read through and complete Session Four in the participant book. Also, if you are using *Spiritual Entrepreneurs* as an additional resource, give the following assignment: Read the Introduction and Chapter 1 of *Spiritual Entrepreneurs*.

4

SESSION FOUR
LORD OF ALL

Prepare for the Session

Supplies Needed
- chalkboard or dry-erase board and markers
- Bibles
- participant books
- pens/pencils

Talk to your pastor or other church leaders to request any printed information they may have regarding your church's belief about baptism, or use the included information on baptism on page 49 (also in participant book, p. 38). Be prepared also to discuss the requirements for membership in your church.

Ice Breaker

Begin this session with prayer. Then walk around the room and observe where participants are sitting. At random, ask several people to swap places, moving from one table to another. Do not offer any explanation as to why. After you have moved several people, randomly ask a few people to stand. Again, offer no explanation. If anyone questions the requests, just say that you need them to trust you. Once several people are standing, ask everyone to sit down and discuss these questions within their groups:

- In general, how do you feel about being told what to do?
- What is your reaction to what just happened—being told whether you should stand or where you should sit, without explanation?
- How is your reaction to this experience similar to the way we react to authority in general?
- Why is it sometimes hard for us to submit to authority?

Today we're going to explore several areas related to authority in order to get us thinking about the implications of the profound fact that Jesus is Lord. Using Scripture as a guide, we will explore three areas: the differences between kingdoms and democracies, the differences between bondservants and volunteers, as well as who is in control of our resources. As we discuss each area, keep in mind that the ultimate goal is to answer the question, *What does it mean to make Jesus Lord of my life?*

Group Discussion - Kingdom vs. Democracy

Have the group divide into smaller groups or pairs. Write on the board or flip chart the words "Kingdom" and "Democracy." Ask the class to list ways that kingdoms and democracies are different. Here are some ideas that are also included in the participant book (p. 32):

Democracy

- A democracy is headed by elected leaders who can be changed based on their popularity with people.
- A democracy allows participation by members of that democracy in the decision-making process. The people can change the rules.
- The leadership in a democracy represents the people.

Kingdom

- A king rules on the basis of his birth and is king for life.
- A kingdom is ruled by a king who gives decrees and expects obedience. Approval by the people is not involved.
- In a kingdom, the people represent the king.

Have the members of each group discuss together whether their households constitute democracies or kingdoms. What about their workplaces?

Then ask each group to look up the following verses together and answer the questions: Luke 23:1-3; Matthew 6:9-10; 1 Timothy 6:13-16; Revelation 19:11-16.

- From these verses, is Christianity more like a democracy or a kingdom?
- What does that mean for followers of Jesus?
- In what practical ways is life different because of the absolute authority of Jesus?

After the groups share with the larger group insights from their discussion, remind the class that Jesus came as King of kings and Lord of lords, ruler over all. Being in relationship with Jesus means becoming part of his kingdom and submitting to his rule and authority. This requires obedience to his commands on our part.

Group Discussion - Servant or Volunteer

Have each small group divide up into pairs. In each pair, choose one person to play the role of "Master" and one to play the role of "Servant." For the next three minutes, the servants must do anything the masters tell them to do. The servants may not talk unless asked to speak, nor may they do anything of their own volition. They may do only what their master commands.

Here is a list of possible commands for the masters to give to their servants:

- Get me a drink of water, cup of coffee, etc.
- Organize my handouts and papers for me.
- Check to see what the class in the next room is doing, and bring me a report.
- Tie my shoes.
- Anything creative that is respectful and honors personal space!

After three minutes is up, the roles are no longer to be played. Have group members talk about what just happened by discussing these questions:

- How did it feel to be a servant or a master?
- Why does the idea of being a servant sometimes sound negative?
- What does it mean to be a servant of God? How does that differ from being a volunteer?

Bring the class back together. If you are using *Spiritual Entrepreneurs* as an additional resource, lead a class discussion on Chapter 1, "The Lordship Principle." Ask the class:

- What was the earliest Christian creed? (p. 26)
- What is the New Testament meaning of "Lord"? (p. 36)
- What does the author mean when he states, "Volunteer is the language of the club. Slave is the language of the kingdom of God"? (p. 40)

- How do you feel about the idea of being a servant versus being a volunteer?
- Practically speaking, what does it mean to make Jesus "Lord" of your life?

Share with the class: The thought of being a servant is not normally a pleasing one to us, yet the term Jesus chose to use to describe his followers was *slave* or *servant*. Servanthood represents a loss of control over our lives. We like to say, "I volunteer my time at the church," meaning we feel good about donating some of our time; but we still like to be able to decide our limits, set our boundaries, protect ourselves, and to pick and choose what we will or will not do based on what is convenient for us.

> These verses show the servant language Jesus' followers used in introducing themselves:
>
> Philippians 1:1
> James 1:1
> Revelation 1:1
> Titus 1:1

The original disciples saw themselves as anything but volunteers. As part of a society based on the institution of slavery, they clearly understood a slave's role and a slave's relationship to his or her master. Followers of Jesus like Paul, James, and John used words like *bondservant* and *prisoner* of Christ to describe themselves and to acknowledge Jesus' authority over them (see box). The term *bondservant* has special meaning because bondservants were persons set free from slavery with the option to stay free but who voluntarily put themselves back into the servant role.

The difference between volunteers and servants is a matter of mindset. While issues like convenience and the ability to choose and control are important to a volunteer, a servant has no agenda but that of his or her master.

The word summing up how we submit to Jesus' authority is *obedience*. While most of us are determined to be independent and make our own decisions, Jesus makes it clear that to love him means to follow him with single-minded obedience. Listen to Jesus' words from John 14:15: "If you love me, keep my commands."

Coming to Jesus is not just a continuation of life as it has been with the addition of God's blessing; rather, it is a life of submitting to Jesus' authority and doing what Jesus tells us to do. Obedience is more than lip service. It is a way of life in which we are no longer self-ruling individuals. God rules everything in our lives.

Group Discussion - Who Is in Control?

This is an exercise dealing with the control of your resources. Refer participants to the exercise in their participant books (pp. 34–36), which is reproduced below. Have small groups go through this exercise together.

Tell the class: Using the spaces provided, write down in the first column the five most valuable resources you possess. These may be material or financial possessions but could also include less tangible items such as time, talents, career, family, and other relationships. Next to each item, write in the second column the name of the person or institution that presently has authority and control over that resource. For example, if the resource is your house, the institution in authority over it may be the bank. If a person is listed as a valuable resource, that person probably is the authority over himself or herself. If time or talent is listed, the authority may be you. When everyone is finished writing, share what you wrote with the rest of your group.

1. _____ _____ _____
2. _____ _____ _____
3. _____ _____ _____
4. _____ _____ _____
5. _____ _____ _____

Read Acts 2:42-47 and 4:32-35, and have participants respond to the following questions.

- What do these verses say about the way the early disciples viewed their personal resources?
- Who do you think was in control of the disciples' resources?
- What were the results of this community putting their resources under Jesus' control?

Tell the class: For each item you wrote down, cross out the name of the person or institution that you listed in the second column as being in control of that resource; and write "Jesus Christ" in its place in the third column. Then write a description of how your life might be different if you gave Jesus total control of each of the resources you listed. When everyone is finished writing, those who wish may share what they wrote with the rest of the group. Don't pressure anyone who is uncomfortable with sharing. Identify in the discussion what seem to be the most important resources and where discomfort lies in surrendering them to Jesus. Did anyone feel a sense of peace from giving up control?

Trusting Jesus as Lord

Have a class member read aloud Matthew 7:21-27. Then ask:
- Why do you think Jesus wants to be Lord of your life?
- How would relinquishing control of your life to God benefit you?
- What's the main thing that hinders you from letting Jesus be Lord of your life?

To make Jesus "Lord" means to give him control over everything in our lives—all that we do, all that we own, all that we are. We live in an affluent society with an individualistic mentality, so giving up control is a major issue. We may feel uncomfortable or even fearful in handing Jesus control of our lives, but let's remember to whom we are giving control.

Read Matthew 11:28-30 to the class, then ask the question, "What will you find when you give Jesus control?" This passage tells us of a master who wants to ease our load, not make our load heavier. Our trust in Jesus grows as we come to know him and understand his character and his loving intentions toward us.

Reflection

Have participants move their chairs away from everyone else and sit quietly with their eyes closed. Help them reflect on what it means to be in a relationship with Jesus, then conclude with a prayer for God to be given complete authority in each participants' life.

You might use words like this: "As we welcome Jesus into our lives and into our hearts, we enter into a relationship with him. We accept and relate to him as both Savior and Lord. If Jesus is Lord, then he has absolute authority over all areas of our lives. Think of the different areas of your life—your family, work, friends, health, finances, job, even hobbies. We cannot compartmentalize our lives, giving him authority over only one or two areas and keeping the rest for ourselves. What would it look like if you truly gave God authority over your life through Jesus Christ?

"Take these next moments to be silent and allow Jesus to show you where you need to let him be Lord. As he shows you each area of your life that you need to let him control, surrender that area to him, and then pray for him to have complete authority in your life."

Closing Prayer

Lord Jesus, I thank you for being in control of all things—including my life. I offer you the areas of my life that I have not surrendered to you; transform them to honor you. Strengthen me in living under your Lordship. Thank you for your care for me.

Homework

Ask the class to read the information on baptism (Leader Guide, p. 49; participant book, p. 38) and to bring any questions they have to their study leader. Also, ask them to read and complete Session Five.

What Is Baptism?

Baptism, in some form, is a requirement for membership for many denominations. Baptism is a public statement of your entry into a personal relationship with Jesus Christ. It is the outward *sign* of your salvation, not its *source*. There are at least three ways of addressing baptism. Ask your study leader or pastor about baptism at your church.

Elements of Baptism

1. Recognition of baptism as an infant or young child is an acknowledgment of the faith statement made by parents or guardians on a child's behalf. It affirms that God is involved and active in the child's life. An adult who was baptized as an infant or child is not required to be baptized again.
2. Baptism of a new believer as a sign of your new relationship with Jesus Christ. This is done in two ways:
   a. Sprinkling. This method involves having water dripped over your head by a pastor during a baptism service.
   b. Immersion. This method involves being totally submerged under water. A pastor does this during a baptism service.
3. Reaffirmation of baptism. This applies to persons who have already been baptized, but desire to make a public statement of faith concerning their deeper relationship or renewed commitment with Christ. A pastor places the sign of the cross on the person's forehead.

Part 2
Growing in the Spirit

5

SESSION FIVE
The Holy Spirit

Prepare for the Session

Supplies Needed
- chalkboard or dry-erase board and markers
- Bibles
- participant books
- pens/pencils
- "Three in One" video OR boiling water in a thermos, room temperature water in a glass, ice in a cooler, and a hard-boiled egg

A video series on the Trinity is available to you on the Ginghamsburg UMC website (http://ginghamsburg.org/followingjesus). The sermons from Michael Slaughter titled "Trinity: The Unity Factor" and "Powerful Presence: God the Spirit" provide helpful background for talking with participants about the content of today's lesson. Also available is a five-minute video called "Three in One" that can be downloaded and shown to the class. This video helps explain the Trinity through the use of water and eggs as models.

If you are not using the "Three in One" video, bring to class boiling water in a thermos, ice cubes in a small cooler, a glass of water, and a hard-boiled egg.

What Are the Characteristics of the Holy Spirit?

In the last few sessions we've been talking about who Jesus is. Most of us have a pretty good understanding of who God the Father is and the relationship between the Father and the Son. However, when we add the Holy Spirit to the conversation, we sometimes become confused. Using models such as water or an egg helps us understand how God can be Father, Son, and Holy Spirit—and yet remain one God. **(If using the "Three in One" video, show it here.)**

Illustrations of the Trinity

Scripturally, the Trinity is revealed as three distinct persons in relationship with one another who coexist as one Godhead—a true mystery. Explain briefly how the models you have provided help us understand God's three-in-one identity: One illustration of this is water in three forms—liquid, ice, and steam. Each form coexists with the others, but is separate and distinct from the others. All three forms have the same chemical equation—H_2O—that remains constant no matter what form the water takes. Likewise the egg is made up of three distinct parts: the yolk, the white, and the shell. Each part looks different and has a distinct purpose; but at the most basic level, all three have the DNA of egg. The three persons of God are separate and distinct from each other, yet have the same nature and attributes. At the core, all three are equally God.

The Trinity is mysterious and not easy to understand, but it is critical to our faith. It has been said, "The person who tries to understand the Trinity will surely lose his mind . . . but the person who denies the Trinity will surely lose his soul."

In this session, our goal is to answer two questions: *Who is the Holy Spirit?* and *What is the Spirit's role in our lives?*

Group Discussion

Have participants form two groups. Have each person in one group refer to "The Holy Spirit Personality Profile" exercise on page 42 of the participant book. Tell the class that in this exercise we are looking for characteristics of a personality or personhood. These characteristics remind us that we are relating to the Holy Spirit as a person rather than an undefined, formless entity. Refer each person in the other group to the "Role of the Holy Spirit" exercise on page 44 of the participant book. The Scriptures included in this exercise help us identify the role the Holy Spirit plays in our lives and in the world. Ask participants to work together to complete their assignment and prepare to present their findings to the whole group.

Have your groups reconnect and share what they've discovered about the Holy Spirit. Start with the Scriptures about the characteristics of the person of the Holy Spirit found in the Scriptures below. Some helps are provided if needed.

The Holy Spirit Personality Profile

- Romans 8:27—*Has a mind and an intellect*
- 1 Corinthians 2:9-13—*Has the thoughts of God, words, a language*
- 1 Corinthians 12:11—*Has a will and makes decisions*
- Romans 15:30; Ephesians 4:30; Hebrews 10:29—*Has the full range of emotions*

Matthew 28:19-20 reminds us that the Holy Spirit is God, equal with the Father and the Son. The Spirit has all the attributes and power and wisdom that God possesses. In Scripture, the Holy Spirit is called the Spirit of God and the Spirit of Christ as well as the Holy Spirit. And if you are a follower of Jesus, the Holy Spirit lives within your spirit. It is essential to grasp the fact that the Spirit has the characteristics of a person so that we can understand the reality of our continual personal relationship with God through the Spirit. As we experience the Spirit's personality, we see God and get to know God on a personal level. The Holy Spirit enables believers to know and walk with God by being present, active, and responsive in our lives every day.

> "Therefore go and make disciples of all nations, baptizing them in the name of the Father and of the Son and of the Holy Spirit." (Matthew 28:19)

If you are using *Spiritual Entrepreneurs* as an additional resource, this is a good place to lead a discussion on Chapter 2, "The Biblical Principle." Ask:

- Why did John Wesley consider the Bible to be the last word in determining the boundaries of the Christian faith? (p. 48)
- How does the Bible take us beyond information to transformation in our lives? (p. 54)
- What is the connection between the Bible and the Holy Spirit?

Holy Spirit Movements

As one-third of the Trinity, the Spirit has always been active in God's plan for the world. The Holy Spirit is mentioned all through the Old Testament, from Creation in Genesis 1 through the inspiration of the prophets at the end of the Old Testament. In the Old Testament, the Spirit was available to a few key individuals. For example, we read about the Spirit "coming upon" such people as David and Samson, giving them wisdom and power to do what God had called them to do. However, not everyone had or experienced the Spirit; and, as with King Saul, the Spirit did not always remain long-term with a person.

In the New Testament we can see that Jesus relied on the power of the Spirit during his time on earth. Philippians 2:5-8 tells us that Jesus set aside his power as God when he took on human form:

Have the same attitude of mind Christ Jesus had: Who, being in very nature God, did not consider equality with God something to be used to his own advantage; rather, he made himself nothing by taking the very nature of a servant, being made in human likeness. And being found in appearance as a human being, he humbled himself by becoming obedient to death—even death on a cross!

The New Testament makes frequent references to Jesus being "full of the Spirit" as he fulfilled his ministry. Jesus lived his life on earth just as we have to live; he showed us how to depend on the Spirit moment by moment.

There is a distinct difference in how the Spirit acted between the Old Testament and the New Testament. In the New Testament, after Jesus' resurrection and ascension, the Spirit became available to everyone who is in a personal relationship with Jesus. Now, all followers of Jesus have the same power that was available to the greats of the Old Testament. However, instead of the Spirit "coming upon" people, now the Spirit lives within people. The Holy Spirit is present and active in our lives to empower us, but it's our choice as to how much we will allow the Spirit to do that.

Now let's talk about the role of the Holy Spirit in our lives as Christians and in the world. Ask the groups working on these Scriptures to share what they discovered. Some helps are provided below.

Role of the Holy Spirit

- John 14:25-26—*Teaches and reminds us of Jesus and his word*
- John 15:26—*The Spirit of Truth who testifies of / tells about Jesus*
- John 16:7-11—*Our Advocate who also convicts believers and the world of sin*
- John 16:12-15—*Glorifies Jesus and makes the things of Jesus known*
- Acts 1:8—*Gives us power as Christ's witnesses and for ministry*
- Romans 8:14-17—*Assures us of our relationship with Christ*
- 1 Corinthians 6:19-20—*Lives within us*

- 1 Corinthians 12:7-11—*Gives us spiritual gifts and equips each of us uniquely to serve*
- Galatians 5:16-23—*Gives us power over our tendency to sin and shapes us into the character of Christ*

Filled With the Spirit

Ask the class, "What is the difference between *having* the Holy Spirit and being *filled with* the Spirit?" Use the following verses to help clarify answers.

Ask individuals to read aloud each of the following Scriptures, then discuss each Scripture's insight and meaning:

- Acts 2:38—*When we repent and are baptized in the name of Jesus Christ, our sins are forgiven; and we receive the gift of the Holy Spirit.*
- Romans 8:9—*Anyone who does not have the Spirit of Christ does not belong to Christ.*

"Live by the Spirit, I say, and do not gratify the desires of the flesh. For what the flesh desires is opposed to the Spirit, and what the Spirit desires is opposed to the flesh; for these are opposed to each other, to prevent you from doing what you want. But if you are led by the Spirit, you are not subject to the law." (Galatians 5:16-18, NRSV)

The definition of a follower of Jesus is one who has the Spirit of God living in him or her, and this happens at the moment we open our lives to Jesus. So, all followers of Jesus have the Holy Spirit living within them. However, the filling of the Spirit is accomplished only when we choose to give up control over our own lives and allow the Holy Spirit to control and empower us.

As time allows, ask participants to either read the following verses aloud to the group or have small groups read and discuss these examples of Spirit-filled Christians from Scripture:

- Acts 4:8-13
- Acts 4:31-35
- Galatians 5:16-26

We see dramatic effects on everyday people as a result of their choice to let the Spirit lead and empower them.

In Acts 4, ordinary fishermen were used to powerfully speak the truth of Jesus as the result of the filling of the Spirit. God uses people regardless of their background, even without formal education or training. God wants people who are simply surrendered to the Holy Spirit. Acts 4 also shows that being controlled and empowered by the Spirit changes entire communities. The first century church, rather than focusing on themselves and their needs, became other-centered and took care of one another. The Scripture says they gave as each had need, and their community ended up with no one in need (verses 32-35). Their example won many others to Jesus.

> "By contrast, the fruit of the Spirit is love, joy, peace, patience, kindness, generosity, faithfulness, gentleness, and self-control. There is no law against such things. And those who belong to Christ Jesus have crucified the flesh with its passions and desires. If we live by the Spirit, let us also be guided by the Spirit." (Galatians 5:22-25, NRSV)

Galatians 5:22-25 speaks of how our character will change when we allow the Spirit to control instead of ourselves. The character of Christ, referred to as the fruit of the Spirit in these verses, begins to emerge in such a distinct way that people will look at us, see Jesus, and be drawn to him.

Galatians 5:16-18 tells us that we are a walking battleground between our human nature, which always defaults to sin, and the presence of the Spirit, which always takes us God's way. We have the power to overcome sin through the Spirit living within us; we make the choice as to whom we give power. As we choose to live by the power of the Spirit, Jesus wins! We will not be controlled by our old nature but will say, think, and do what God wants us to do.

This internal battle is real, and we will find ourselves dealing with choices all day long. Sometimes our choices do not please God. God is involved in the process of transformation, making changes in us, big or small, every day until we are formed in the image of Christ. God uses our choices to teach and form us.

The Process of Filling

A metaphor created by Bill Bright, founder of Campus Crusade for Christ, helps visualize how we deal with our daily choices and is called "spiritual breathing." Think of the physical process of breathing, which keeps us alive. It consists of a rhythm between exhaling, which rids the body of waste products, and inhaling, which provides clean oxygen for our body's use. We need both to live. The spiritual application is the rhythm between confession (exhaling the toxic waste of our spiritual life by agreeing with God that we have gone our own way and done what is displeasing to God) and inhaling (asking the Holy Spirit to fill up all the spaces opened up through confession). We need both to keep our spiritual life going. As we grow, both physically and spiritually, our respiration rate changes. When you watch a baby sleeping you realize babies have the fastest respiration rate of the human family; they breathe quickly and lightly. But, as life goes on, our respiration tends to slow, especially as we train and develop ourselves. Any highly trained athlete will have a slow and steady breathing rate because their body and its organs are in such great condition and operate efficiently. The same is true as we train and condition ourselves spiritually. The more we focus on being with God through Bible study, prayer, journaling, meditation, service, and other spiritual disciplines, the more we train ourselves to be aware of God and our connection with God. Our confession and filling rate slow down because we will be controlled and empowered by the Spirit for longer periods of time.

Reflection

Being filled with the Holy Spirit establishes Jesus as Lord of our lives. In what area of your life do you feel the Spirit moving? In what area do you need to let the Spirit more fully control and empower you?

Closing Prayer

Thank you, God, for being such a personal God and choosing to live within me. Thank you for your goodness in supplying through the Holy Spirit all the resources I need to live life as you intend. I confess that I have taken control of my life and strayed from what you have desired for me. Now I breathe in the fullness of your love and forgiveness. Holy Spirit, fill me and make me new once again.

Homework

Before dismissing the group, remind participants to complete the "Spiritual Fruit Inventory" on pages 47–51 in the participant book (also on pp. 62–66 of this Leader Guide) before the next session. Ask class members to also read and complete Session Six.

Spiritual Fruit Inventory: Evaluating Your Spiritual Fruit

Most of us know how to evaluate fruit to tell whether it is good or bad to eat. There is also a way to evaluate how well we express the fruit of the Spirit in our lives. You can gauge your effectiveness in allowing the fruit of the Spirit to be demonstrated in your life by answering the following questions. When you are finished, tally your score to see which character qualities appear to be most evident in your life.

Based on your personal experience, respond to the following statements. Use the number system below to rank each statement in the space provided next to each question.

0 = Never true for me   2 = True most of the time
1 = True every once in a while   3 = Definitely true for me

____ 1. I am grateful that God loved the world (and me!) so much that God's Son was sacrificed as our means of salvation.

____ 2. God's presence makes me glad.

____ 3. I rest in the fact that God is in control of all things—past, present, and future.

____ 4. Even though I don't always understand what's happening, I am willing to wait on God to act on my behalf.

____ 5. I am amazed by God's intense care for me shown by sending Jesus to take the punishment I deserve.

____ 6. I know that there are times when God is justified in being angry.

____ 7. I love the fact that Jesus set aside his power as God in order to reach out to broken and hurting people.

____ 8. I know that God will do exactly what God promises.

____ 9. My lifestyle reflects my obedience to God.

____ 10. I'm confident in God's love for me, even when I act in an unloving way toward others.

____ 11. I have an inner assurance of my relationship with Jesus.

____12. Because I have Jesus, I am calmer, even when problems come along.

____13. I accept others right where they are.

____14. I choose to forgive others because Jesus chooses to forgive me.

____15. I am immediately sensitive to the conviction of God's Spirit when I've done something wrong.

____16. When someone approaches me in anger, I generally don't react with the same harshness.

____17. People who know me well would say that I have a consistent walk with God.

____18. I say no to things that might hinder my communion with God.

____19. I am committed to serving others, even when I don't feel like it.

____20. Even when things go wrong, I have an inner assurance of God's presence.

____21. I am confident that my sins are forgiven.

____22. I don't complain about my problems; instead, I trust God.

____23. I comfort, encourage, and affirm others.

____24. I live a lifestyle that pleases God.

____25. Even when I feel attacked, I am committed to obeying God's Word and submitting to the Holy Spirit.

____26. I follow through with what I say I will do.

____27. I am committed to a consistent time alone with God for prayer and Bible study.

____28. I choose to be positive and affirm the good qualities of people, even when they get on my nerves.

____29. I have consistent satisfaction from doing what God wants me to do.

____30. I am confident that God accepts me because of my relationship with Jesus.

____31. I am content that God has me in process and will develop me into what God wants me to be.

____32. I speak positively to others to build them up.

____33. I am truthful, honest, and keep the promises I make.

___34. I seek to be humble, cooperative, and teachable all the time.

___35. I am responsible.

___36. I have asked my friends or a support group to hold me accountable for areas in which I struggle.

___37. I serve others with no expectations of being served in return.

___38. I have a deep sense of pleasure because I sense God's presence as I serve.

___39. I am not easily stressed out because I know God is in control.

___40. I am willing to wait for things that will benefit me physically, spiritually, or materially.

___41. I listen and try to understand others.

___42. I have confronted other Christians in a caring way when they have made wrong choices in the way they live.

___43. I am open and receptive to feedback in areas in which I need improvement.

___44. I use the abilities God has given me for God's glory.

___45. When I recognize a behavior problem in my life, I immediately act to bring it under control.

___46. When I have been hurt, I am willing to forgive and begin again with that person.

___47. I delight in what God is doing in the lives of others.

___48. I have a calm assurance even in difficult situations.

___49. When I am hurting, I place my hope in God.

___50. I am compassionate and respond to the needs of others.

___51. I am involved in serving others in my community and around the world in order to influence others for Jesus.

___52. Regardless of my feelings, I focus on doing what is right.

___53. Because I belong to God, I understand that my time, money, and energy are God's to use as God wishes.

___54. Distractions do not keep me from my goals.

___55. I pray for my enemies and for those who are difficult to love.

___56. No matter what I am doing, I am content because God is with me and is using me to serve others.

___57. I experience the Holy Spirit's comfort in the midst of the world's chaos.

___58. I accept others who are different from me.

___59. I treat others with kindness and generosity, even when they are different from me or rejected by others.

___60 I take a stand for truth and against injustice.

___61. I don't seek revenge when others hurt me.

___62. My friends know they can count on me.

___63. I stay away from situations in which I am easily tempted.

After completing the Inventory, place your answer beside each corresponding question number in the table on the next page.

Place your answer beside each corresponding question number in the table. Add the total in each horizontal row for your final score. There is a total possible score of 21 for each aspect of the fruit of the Spirit. The higher your score for each quality, the more likely you are to be demonstrating that quality in your life.

							Total	Fruit
1___	10___	19___	28___	37___	46___	55___	A___	Love
2___	11___	20___	29___	38___	47___	56___	B___	Joy
3___	12___	21___	30___	39___	48___	57___	C___	Peace
4___	13___	22___	31___	40___	49___	58___	D___	Patience
5___	14___	23___	32___	41___	50___	59___	E___	Kindness
6___	15___	24___	33___	42___	51___	60___	F___	Goodness
7___	16___	25___	34___	43___	52___	61___	G___	Gentleness
8___	17___	26___	35___	44___	53___	62___	H___	Faithfulness
9___	18___	27___	36___	45___	54___	63___	I___	Self-Control

6

SESSION SIX
FRUIT OF THE SPIRIT

Prepare for the Session

Supplies Needed
- chalkboard or dry-erase board and markers
- Bibles
- participant books
- pens/pencils
- nine different types of fruit—The amount of each fruit will be determined by the number of people in your class. You need enough to make a fruit salad that will serve the entire class. It's okay to divide the fruit up and ask class members to bring assigned fruit with them. (examples: apples, oranges, pears, bananas, grapes, kiwis, pineapple, strawberries, and melon)
- knives, cutting boards, a bowl, paper towels for each small group
- large bowl and serving spoon
- small bowls and utensils to eat the fruit salad

Participants will be taking the "Spiritual Fruit Inventory" before coming to Session Six. It would be helpful for you to take the evaluation yourself in order to help with interpretation. Help the group understand that any evaluation is an attempt to spark self-examination, motivate spiritual growth, and foster discussion. It's not a diagnosis!

During this class, each group will be working with different types of fruit. At the end of the class discussion, each group will contribute their cut up fruit to create a large fruit salad that will serve as a snack for the entire class.

Ice Breaker

Ask each person to think of their very favorite fruit and then have a few people share which fruit they like and what about that fruit makes it their favorite.

Or if you are using *Spiritual Entrepreneurs* as an additional resource, lead participants to discuss Chapter 3 of *Spiritual Entrepreneurs*. Ask:
- From what we have been learning so far in class, from what you have been reading in *Spiritual Entrepreneurs*, and from your own experience, what makes worship a vital experience?
- What attracts people to a worship celebration?
- Why do they want to return?

Finding the Fruit of the Spirit in Yourself

Open with prayer. Share with the class that in a Christian's life, there is an expectation that as we grow in our life of faith, we will begin to produce "fruit," or demonstrate results of living in Christ. As we give control over to the Holy Spirit living within us, the same results that Jesus demonstrated through his life will be produced in our own. We will see two different things happen:

1. We will produce fruit by impacting other people in such a way that they will be drawn to Jesus and into their own personal relationship with him.

2. The fruit of the Spirit listed in Galatians 5:22-23 will be developed in our lives, resulting in the character of Christ shining through us. Our lives will reflect Jesus to those around us.

These two kinds of fruit are interrelated. People are attracted to a Christ-like lifestyle. People around us may even say to us, "You're different. I want what you have."

Lifestyle in the Spirit

Ask three group members to read aloud one of the verses below to the rest of the class. Have the class identify what each passage says about fruit.
- John 15:1-8
- Luke 6:43-45
- Galatians 5:22-23

The fruit of the Spirit you read about in Galatians 5:22-23 is not something we receive. Rather, it is a cluster of character qualities that are progressively produced in us through a life constantly yielded to the Holy Spirit. It is the work of the Holy Spirit in us, not something we produce ourselves. Any fruit bearing is a growing and maturing process in which the fruit takes on the qualities of the parent plant. As long as the fruit is attached to its source of life, the parent plant, it grows and becomes more and more visible. Our responsibility is to stay connected to our source of life and make conscious choices to yield and obey. As we grow and mature, over time we take on the qualities of our heavenly parent in increasingly more visible ways.

Lifestyle is an important issue in Christianity because of the far-reaching impact our lives have on others. Gandhi, known as the George Washington of India, was a Hindu—yet he was very familiar with Christianity. He has been quoted as saying he was extremely attracted to the person of Jesus. But he never converted to Christianity because of Christians, who he experienced to be so unlike their Christ. Obviously, the fruit of the Spirit in our lives impacts our ability to influence others for Jesus.

What Is the Fruit of the Spirit

The fruit of the Spirit is not the same as the gifts of the Spirit. We will discuss in detail the gifts of the Spirit in Session Seven. What we need to know right now is that spiritual gifts are special empowerments for ministry. They are given to equip and build up the body of Christ. The gifts are what we do. The fruit of the Spirit is a grouping of character qualities in the life of each follower of Jesus. The fruit is who we are. No follower of Jesus is given all the spiritual gifts, but all of the nine character qualities listed in Galatians are to be evident in every follower's life.

Group Discussion

Divide the class into smaller groups. Depending on the size of the class, have a portion of nine different fruit on each table, along with a knife, cutting board, and paper towels. Have them cut up the fruit to be part of a fruit salad as they discuss the spiritual fruit listed on page 56 of the participant book (Leader Guide, pp. 71–72). Make sure you have enough of each fruit to make a salad large enough to feed the entire class. Don't identify the specific spiritual fruit (love, kindness, patience, etc.), but let the group identify both the fruit and the way this characteristic might be exhibited in the life of a Christian.

Allow about ten to fifteen minutes for the groups to read the text, identify the fruits, and discuss the applications. For smaller classes, or to help manage time, it's okay for the groups to use just the first two Scriptures listed for each fruit. Call the groups back together to talk about what they found. Have a representative from each group bring their fruit to combine with fruit from the other groups to make the fruit salad.

The following material is to guide the small groups in their investigation of each fruit of the Spirit. Refer the class to page 56 in the participant book.

Emphasize to participants the importance of applying the information they are gathering about the fruit of the Spirit in their lives. Have them give examples of how we see these characteristics exhibited in daily life or how they personally have experienced one or more of these characteristics in their own lives.

Tell participants: For each of the Scripture groupings below, identify the fruit of the Spirit described. Then discuss as a group how this characteristic might be exhibited in the life of a Christian. Feel free to use your own personal examples or examples of people you know.

Characteristic 1:
Luke 6:32-36; John 3:16-17;
John 13:34-35; 1 John 4:19-21

Characteristic 2:
John 15:9-11; Acts 13:49-52;
Romans 14:17-18; Romans 15:13

Characteristic 3:
Isaiah 32:14-20; John 16:29-33;
Philippians 4:4-7; Romans 5:1-2

Characteristic 4:
Colossians 3:12-13; 2 Timothy 4:1-5;
Ephesians 4:1-2; 1 Thessalonians 5:14-15

Characteristic 5:
Romans 2:1-4; Ephesians 2:4-7;
Romans 11:22-23; Ephesians 4:32

Characteristic 6:
Romans 15:14-16; Ephesians 5:8-11;
2 Peter 1:3-4; Titus 2:11-15

Characteristic 7:
1 Corinthians 4:1-2; 3 John 2-5;
Matthew 25:14-23; Lamentations 3:22-24

Characteristic 8:
Matthew 11:28-30; Titus 3:1-2;
1 Corinthians 4:18-21; 1 Peter 3:13-16

Characteristic 9:
2 Timothy 3:1-5; 1 Timothy 1:7;
Titus 1:7-9; 1 Peter 5:8-11

Defining Fruit of the Spirit

Use the following material to add to the class discussion on each of the fruit of the Spirit.

Love: the ability to unconditionally accept and love others based in this same quality offered to us by God through Jesus Christ; the ability to give ourselves in service to others without expecting anything in return.

Luke 6:32-36; John 3:16-17;
John 13:34-35; 1 John 4:19-21

Love in the New Testament sense is not necessarily a feeling or emotion; it is action. Love is choosing the right and appropriate action toward another, even when you don't feel like it, and expecting nothing in return. This unconditional love is impossible for humans but is accomplished by allowing God to love through us.

Joy: a deep, inner gladness that results from an intimate relationship with Christ. It is maintained through obedience and is renewed through service to others. Joy is not dependent on circumstances but is a result of our communion with God.

John 15:9-11; Acts 13:49-52;
Romans 14:17-18; Romans 15:13

Joy is not just happiness or feeling good; those emotions depend on our circumstances and what is going on around us. Joy is what is produced within us as a result of living in obedience to Christ and prioritizing and serving others. Jesus demonstrated that we can have joy regardless of our circumstances—including suffering. Joy is produced in us as we focus on God and the end result God is bringing about in our lives, not on what we are experiencing. God allows different circumstances in our lives in order for us to learn and to be part of God's transformation process. Jesus did not focus on the pain of the cross, but on the joyful end result of reconnecting us to the Father. As Nehemiah said, the joy of the LORD becomes our strength (Nehemiah 8:10).

Peace: an inner harmony and sense of well-being based on our confident faith that God has accepted us, loves us, and is in control of our lives, no matter how turbulent our external situation might be.

Isaiah 32:14-20; John 16:29-33;
Philippians 4:4-7; Romans 5:1-2

Peace results from knowing we are forgiven and accepted by God. Peace does not require the absence of conflict or distress; it is a sense of tranquility and order regardless of what is happening around us because no matter our circumstances, God has everything in place and is in control. Peace is the internal assurance that no matter how the waves of life rock our boat, Jesus is in the boat with us.

Patience: the ability to exercise restraint and calmly persevere in waiting on God, despite people or circumstances that might provoke us or cause agitation.

Colossians 3:12-13; 2 Timothy 4:1-5;
Ephesians 4:1-2; 1 Thessalonians 5:14-15

Patience is the ability to walk through life long-term, realizing God has a timetable for each process in our lives. Patience accepts consequences, endures the wrong of others, bears injuries and suffering for God, and refuses to retaliate. Being patient does not mean we are to deny our feelings, nor does it mean we cannot set boundaries with others. It does mean we have persistence and staying power. Patience is hard! Let's face it, other people and life situations get under our skin. Patience is not a quality that comes naturally or easily for us. Patience is part of God's character and can only become our character through God's power and Spirit working in us.

Kindness: the ability to treat others with openness, sensitivity, and love—especially those who have specific needs we can meet. This ability is based on the kindness shown to us by God.

Romans 2:1-4; Ephesians 2:4-7;
Romans 11:22-23; Ephesians 4:32

Kindness deals not with our abilities but our attitudes. We can be extremely gifted in skills; yet our style, tone, and volume of voice can be hurtful. Kindness is the Christ-like way we treat others, and includes attitudes like compassion, mercy, friendliness, and loyalty. We demonstrate kindness through the Spirit's power and because God has demonstrated kindness to us.

Goodness: to have the nature of God, and therefore, to be able to discern right from wrong, do good to others, and expose evil and injustice.

Romans 15:14-16; Ephesians 5:8-11;
2 Peter 1:3-4; Titus 2:11-15

Goodness results from the Spirit developing within us the same sense of right and wrong God has. Loving confrontation comes from this character quality. Goodness may be expressed as taking a stand against wrong in the lives of others or in society. Goodness must always work hand-in-hand with kindness. Goodness boldly calls people to account-ability. Kindness tempers our attitude in confrontation. Kindness without goodness can become co-dependence, but goodness without kindness can result in unnecessary harshness and judgment. Jesus used both goodness and kindness in his confrontation with the Samaritan woman in John 4. He dealt with her serial adultery head-on but lov-ingly related to her at the same time.

Faithfulness: an unshakable loyalty displayed by being trustwor-thy, reliable, and responsible: completely carrying out commitments to God and others.

1 Corinthians 4:1-2; 3 John 2-5;
Matthew 25:14-23; Lamentations 3:22-24

Faithfulness means following through and fulfilling promises we make. Our commitment level is determined by this character quality. God is a God of covenant, or unbreakable promises, and is willing to stick with us regardless of our behavior or circumstances. God promises to never walk away from us, as Hebrews 13:5 assures us. Because this covenantal God lives within us, we are empowered to be faithful, too, in all our relationships and commitments.

Gentleness: demonstrating consideration and thoughtfulness—putting my rights and strength willingly under God's control in order to handle myself in a calm manner. Gentleness requires openness, humility, and a teachable spirit, rather than the harshness originating from personal pride and selfishness.

Matthew 11:28-30; Titus 3:1-2;
1 Corinthians 4:18-21; 1 Peter 3:3-16

Gentleness is revealed through cooperation, humility, and accountability. A gentle person is not a weak person; rather, this person has put their strength under the control of God. Like a tamed horse, that strength is now useful and focused. A gentle person may act with feeling or tough decisiveness, yet they are under control. In Matthew 5:5, Jesus blesses the gentle (meek).

 Self-control: to take responsibility for myself and exercise discipline in order to avoid sin and live a life that pleases God.

*2 Timothy 3:1-5; 1 Timothy 1:7;
Titus 1:7-9; 1 Peter 5:8-11*

Self-control is a choice to give God control over our lives. This results in a lifestyle that is appealing to God, and brings us the support and power of the Holy Spirit to prevent or overcome excesses. As we study Scripture and pray we learn and understand God's principles and teachings. We also come to know the limitations God puts on such things as the use of the tongue, sex, excessive eating and drinking, anger, and other issues. We are able to model after people in Scripture who were empowered by the Spirit to avoid committing what is expressly forbidden in Scripture. Ultimately self-control is Spirit-control.

Reflection - Spiritual Fruit Inventory

Check in with the class to see how many of the group members completed the evaluation (participant book, pp. 47–51) during the week. (Assess whether you need to allot a few minutes for this exercise.) Ask the group to divide into pairs or trios and discuss their results. Encourage participants to identify one aspect of spiritual fruit in which they are strong and one that needs work. Ask the group to end their conversation with prayer for each other that the Holy Spirit will work through them to display the fruit of the Spirit more powerfully in their lives.

As you serve the fruit salad snack to your class, lead the class in a discussion of how the fruit salad is similar to the fruit of the Spirit in a Christian's life: all the fruit are present and work together; some fruit stand out more than others; some fruit we don't enjoy as much as others, just like some of the fruit of the Spirit are more of a challenge to develop than others. The fruit salad also is similar to Christians working together to do God's will, each bringing a flavor, nourishment, and texture to the community.

Developing Your Fruit

The most important thing that you can communicate to the group is that we are all a work in process. Say, "The example in your books used an apple, growing from a blossom to a beautiful red fruit to describe the way we develop in Christ-likeness. It's not always a perfect progression—in fact it usually is not. We have good days and bad, times when we are growing and feel like we are progressing—and times when we feel stuck."

The wonderful truth about the Christian life is we are all on a progressive journey. Each of us demonstrates the fruit of the Spirit differently and will grow at different rates. It is similar to the development of an apple. In the spring, blossoms form on the apple trees and are soon pollinated. The blossoms fade and dry up, and are replaced with the bud of an apple. Over weeks and months the bud develops into a little green apple, which grows in size and color. By fall, the apple is red and lusciously sweet, ready to be picked. The apple is exactly what God had in mind. Each of us is in one of the developmental stages of the apple. Some of us are just budding, others are little green apples, and some are developing the color and sweetness of mature fruit. Every stage of development is essential and is necessary for the next stage to happen. Even if we are little hard, sour apples right now, we are right where God wants and needs us to be. We can't grow bigger and better without being where we are now. It is important for the little green apple to stay attached to its parent plant so it can come to full growth. Likewise, it is important for us to stay attached to Jesus for us to ripen and mature into the people God has in mind, demonstrating the fruit of God's presence in our lives.

Closing Prayer

Thank you, God, for being the source of my life and growth, the vine to which I seek to stay attached. I am so thankful for your investment in my transformation process. May your character qualities increasingly grow in me and may those around me increasingly see Jesus through me.

Homework

Next week, the class will focus on spiritual gifts. They are to read and complete Session Seven in the participant book. Direct the class members to either one of the listed online gift inventories or distribute an inventory, in print. Their assessment is to be completed by next session. Some helpful spiritual gift inventories are available from:

- www.gregwiens.com/gifts
- http://www.umc.org/site/c.lwL4KnN1LtH/b.1355371/k.9501/Spiritual_Gifts.htm
- http://archive.elca.org/evangelizingchurch/assessments/spiritgifts.html
- For a hardcopy assessment, see *Breakthru: A Spiritual Gifts Diagnostic Inventory* by Ralph Ennis (call 919-783-0354 or visit http://www.leadconsulting-usa.com) or *Serving From the Heart* by Yvonne Gentile and Carol Cartmill (Abingdon, 2002, 2007).

7

SESSION SEVEN
GIFTS OF THE SPIRIT

Prepare for the Session

Supplies Needed
- chalkboard or dry-erase board and markers
- Bibles
- participant books
- pens/pencils

Your participants will be taking a spiritual gifts assessment before coming to this session. Even if you've done this many times before, take the inventory again yourself in order to help with interpretation. Note if you had any surprises that you can share. Help the group understand that, like their "Spiritual Fruit Inventory," any inventory like this is an attempt to spark self-examination and discussion; it's not a diagnosis!

Ice Breaker

Ask the group members to write their names inside the first box on page 63 in their participant books, using their normal writing hand. Then have them change to the other hand and write their name again, this time in the second box. Ask, "How does it feel to do something that was not natural to you?" Ask the group about the legibility of the writing and how much time and energy it took to write with each hand. Ask, "How do you feel about the results?"

Say, "Many people within the church have this same uncomfortable feeling when they try to serve in a way that is not natural to them. And the results can be disastrous! For example: for some people, to serve in an administrative position is absolutely de-energizing. Details frazzle them, and they are not efficient at doing many of the tasks related to the job at hand. Serving in an area for which you are not designed can be uncomfortable, tiring, non-productive, and can eventually lead to burn-out. That is why it's so important to identify who you are and to connect with an area of service that fits with how God has uniquely created you.

God has prepared each of us to serve within the church. Part of this preparation is giving you one or more spiritual gifts. Not all of us are gifted in the same way. God has not used a cookie cutter to stamp out people in a process of uniformity. That's why it feels awkward for you to serve the body of Christ in a way that does not suit how God has designed you and gifted you.

Defining Spiritual Gifts

A spiritual gift is a supernatural power within you to serve others. It is more than a human talent; it is the work of the Holy Spirit in your life, empowering you in a specific way to serve well.

Ask a class member to read aloud the following Scripture passages. As they read, make a list on the board of all the spiritual gifts highlighted in the passages:

- Romans 12:4-8
- 1 Corinthians 12:4-11, 27-31
- Ephesians 4:11-13

To sum up this list of gifts, read 1 Corinthians 12:12-26 to the participants and emphasize the equal need for all gifts and the interrelated nature of gifts.

Some of the gifts are listed once, but others are listed in more than one of these passages. All together there are twenty different gifts mentioned within the three Scripture references. Let's explore these twenty in more detail.

Group Discussion

Have participants form six groups. Using the lists below (also in the participant book on pp. 65–67), assign each group one of the lists of spiritual gifts. They are to discuss the definition of each of their assigned gifts and identify one way they might see that gift operating in the local church. Tell them to be prepared to share their answers with the whole group following their discussion.

GROUP 1

Exhortation (encouragement)—the ability to encourage people and assist them in moving toward spiritual maturity and personal wholeness. This gift uses the skills of comfort and confrontation, encouragement and instruction.

Giving—the ability to give of material wealth freely and with joy to further God's causes. Use of this gift provides physical resources in response to assessed needs.

Leadership—the ability to see "the big picture" and assemble the component parts through the ability to motivate, coordinate, and direct the efforts of others in doing God's work.

GROUP 2

Teaching—the ability to understand and clearly communicate God's truths to others in ways that lead them to apply God's truth to their lives.

Prophecy—the ability to proclaim God's truth in a way that's relevant to current situations and to envision how God would will things to change.

Mercy—the ability to perceive the suffering of others and to minister to them effectively with empathy and without condemnation.

GROUP 3

Serving—demonstrating God's love through the ability to identify the needs of others and selflessly working to meet them.

Wisdom—the ability to understand and apply biblical and spiritual knowledge to practical, everyday problems.

Knowledge—the ability to understand, organize, and effectively use information, from either natural sources or the Holy Spirit directly, for the advancement of God's purposes.

GROUP 4

Faith—the ability to recognize what God wants to accomplish and the steadfast confidence that God will see it done despite what others perceive as barriers.

Healing—the ability to effectively call on God for the curing of illness and the restoration of health in a supernatural way.

Discernment of spirits—the ability to recognize what is of God and what is not of God.

Helps—the ability to work alongside others and see the value of accomplishing practical and often behind-the-scenes tasks that promote God's kingdom.

GROUP 5

Speaking in tongues—the ability to supernaturally speak in a language, known or unknown to others, with no prior knowledge of that language.

Interpretation of tongues—the ability to understand and communicate the words of others who have spoken in tongues, even though the language is unknown.

Pastoring (Shepherding)—the ability to guide and care for a group of Christians as they experience spiritual growth.

GROUP 6

Miracles—the ability to effectively call on God to do supernatural acts that glorify God.

Administration—the ability to organize information, events, or material to work efficiently for the body of Christ.

Apostleship—the ability to see the overall picture and respond by starting new churches, pioneering new ministries that impact multiple churches, or ministering transculturally.

Evangelism—the desire and ability to share the gospel with those who don't know God in a way that provokes them to believe in God.

Fruit and Gifts

There are distinct differences between the fruit of the Spirit that we talked about last week and spiritual gifts. Let's identify those differences.

Create a chart with two columns on the board. On the left side write "Fruit" and on the right side write "Gifts." Ask two participants to go to the board and write facts about the nature of spiritual gifts and spiritual fruit as the other participants call them out. If necessary, have participants refer to page 68 in the participant book, which is reproduced here:

Fruit of the Spirit

All nine character qualities:

- Are present in every believer and are to be developed
- Deal with character—determine who you are
- Develop progressively over time through a lifelong journey
- Are the goal for every Christian
- Define what a Christian is

Gifts of the Spirit

- Are different for every Christian—every believer has a grouping of gifts but not the whole list
- Deal with ministry and serving
- Are given at conversion
- Are the means to reach God's goal for the church
- Determine what a Christian does

Review Ephesians 4:11-16 for the purpose of spiritual gifts. Then say, "Spiritual gifts are special abilities given by the Holy Spirit to equip and build up the body of Christ. Although spiritual gifts are given by God *to you*, the gifts God gives you are not *for you*. They are for the church and are to be used to build up and serve others. It's important to keep in mind that spiritual gifts are not marks of maturity in Christ. Having a spiritual gift does not mean that you are automatically mature in faith. Rather, maturity is measured by how well we express the fruit of the Spirit in our lives."

Make sure participants understand that God cares more about who we are than what we do, and that what we do is birthed out of who we are. The use of our spiritual gifts is impacted by how we let the Spirit control our lives and how we demonstrate Christ-like character.

Group Discussion

Have participants return to their small group and discuss the results of the spiritual gifts inventory that they took during the week. Have each person share with the group their spiritual gifts identified by the inventory and how he or she envisions using those gifts.

Discovering Your Spiritual Gifts

It is important not only to understand what the gifts are but also which specific gifts God has given you. Identifying your own spiritual gifts can really help you find your place of service within the body of Christ. There are four ways you can confirm your spiritual gifts:

1. **Listen to your own heart.** God's will is often revealed through our inner desires and passions. We will have excitement, joy, and anticipation for serving in our gifted area. Remember 1 Corinthians 12 tells us that spiritual gifts can be expressed in different ways, according to our passion and internal wiring. For example, the gift of teaching could be equally effective with adults, children, or youth, through speaking, writing, or media. You will feel energized and fulfilled when functioning in the area intended for you.

2. **Listen to those followers of Jesus who are closest to you.** Often, God will confirm your suspicions about which gifts you have through the observations and opinions of mature Christians God has placed in your life. This underlines the importance of being a part of an authentic, committed community of believers. In this environment we can be honest with each other and be supported in the use of our gifts.

3. **Try out the gift.** God will either confirm your gift or steer you in another direction. This week come up with one way you can test one of the spiritual gifts you identified. For example, if you think you have the gift of exhortation, you could write and send several encouraging cards and letters. Examine the impact of your efforts. Since spiritual gifts are designed to benefit others, you should see positive results as you use your gifts. If you see no results when you experiment with a particular gift, you probably don't have that gift. But that's okay, because there is more than one gift to explore.

4. **The key to identifying and using your spiritual gifts is prayer and more prayer.** The Lord will lead you to accurate discoveries of your gifts if you allow God to guide and direct all your endeavors.

Reflection

Give participants a few moments to be quiet and answer the question:

- How will you implement the use of your spiritual gifts by serving others this week?

Closing Prayer

I thank you, God, for the ways that you are preparing me to serve other people in God's name, and for empowering me to serve others effectively. Guide me in confirming my gifts and using them in ways that will best serve the church.

Homework

Begin lining up a panel of three to four people to speak on spiritual disciplines in Session Nine. It will be helpful to have each person address a different spiritual discipline. Foundational issues to cover are Bible study, prayer, tithing, and service.

Before dismissing the group, ask participants to read and complete Session Eight to be prepared for next week's class. Draw their attention to "Sharing Your Story" on page 72 of the participant book, and ask them to be prepared to share their spiritual journey during the class next week.

8

SESSION EIGHT
SHARING THE SPIRIT

Prepare for the Session

Supplies Needed
- chalkboard or dry-erase board and markers
- Bibles
- participant books
- pens/pencils
- Communion supplies

Arrange with your pastor to have Communion near the end of this week's session.

After an opening prayer and welcome, tell the group that in this session we will share with each other the stories of our spiritual journeys, our experiences with Christ. An important part of being a Christian is sharing your spiritual journey with others as a means of pointing others to a relationship with Jesus or encouraging them in their own walk with Christ. For some of the group this may be a very short journey because they are new in their walk with Christ. For others, the journey will cover a longer period of time. Even people who are still considering whether or not to become a Christian have a story to tell.

The apostle Paul often shared his spiritual journey with others to encourage them to follow God's call in their own lives. As Christians venture out and share how God is working in their lives, they encourage others who might be hesitant or afraid of turning over their life to Christ.

Group Discussion

Using the "Sharing Your Story" exercise on page 91 (also in the participant book, p. 72), have the participants divide into groups of four or six and take turns sharing their spiritual journey with other group members. Rather than focusing on details of their former life, encourage the group members to stay focused on how learning about Jesus or becoming a Christian has transformed their lives. To ensure that everyone has an opportunity to share, it will be important to monitor the time and gently keep participants on track.

Communion

After everyone has had a chance to share their spiritual journey, call the groups back together and share that we'll continue celebrating what Jesus has done for us through sharing Communion together. Ask two participants to read aloud the following Scriptures that relate to the Last Supper, Jesus' resurrection, and Passover:
- Luke 22:7-20
- Luke 24:28-34

Jesus and his disciples met for what would be Jesus' last celebration of Passover or, as it is now called, the Last Supper. At this meal, Jesus shared unleavened bread with his disciples. Traditionally, the unleavened bread was a reminder of Israel's hurried departure from Egypt centuries before, as God miraculously released them from slavery in Egypt. However, during this Last Supper the bread became more. As you heard in the verses from Luke, Jesus said, "This is my body given for you; do this in remembrance of me" (Luke 22:19). He also shared a cup of wine with the disciples and said, "This cup is the new covenant in my blood, which is poured out for you" (Luke 22:20, NIV).

Prepare Yourself

Communion is the most intimate act of the human life—it is where we acknowledge and celebrate our connection with God through Jesus. While sharing bread and wine are symbolic, in some way Jesus actually meets us in the elements.

Communion is not to be entered into lightly. It is not something you "just do," or it becomes simply a ritual. In 1 Corinthians 11, Paul counsels believers to approach Communion with great respect and gratitude. Careful self-evaluation must be done ahead of the taking of the elements, confessing any revealed areas of sin that are separating us from God. Since it is the reminder of the death and resurrection of Jesus and the awesome sacrifice made on our behalf, we must always approach this earnestly and honestly, not taking it for granted.

Stop for a few moments and allow the class to silently do a self-evaluation and have a time of confession and repentance with God. Then say:

"When we share in this meal, we proclaim that we are followers of Jesus. We declare our willingness to join him in spreading love throughout the world, even if it means that we may suffer for it sometimes. We are one with Jesus and his mission. If Jesus unites us, then

Holy Communion is a sacrament, or act of worship, ordained by Christ and is to be observed on a regular basis. All Christians are welcome at our table, whatever their denomination. Communion reminds us of God's great gift of love: God's Son, given for us and all people, his body broken in our place and his blood shed on our behalf. Three essential messages are clear in the Communion service we celebrate: "Christ has died; Christ is risen; Christ will come again."

naturally we must be one with one another. We are all fed from the same loaf and drink from the same cup of God's love. This love unites us with God and with each other, so the meal is called Communion, meaning 'united with.'"

In the last verses from Luke 24, the risen Christ broke bread with two of his followers at Emmaus, "then their eyes were opened, and they recognized him" (24:31, NIV). So, as we are nourished by this meal, our eyes are opened and we recognize Christ in our lives, in our congregation, in our community, and in our world. Our response is thanksgiving—or in Greek, *Eucharisteas*, "gave thanks."

Reflection - Communion Together

Invite the group to celebrate Communion together now in the style that your congregation most often uses.

Closing Prayer

I praise you, God, for each person in my study group (name them individually now). Thank you for each person's presence and impact in the group. Thank you for what you are doing in them and through them. I claim your promise to be with each of us as we seek to share our spiritual journey with others this week.

Homework

Ask class members to read and complete Session Nine in the participant book.

Homework

Sharing Your Story

When you share your spiritual journey with others, it is always helpful to organize your thoughts by writing out what you want to say. Aim to share enough information to fill four to five minutes. Begin by following these steps:

1. Share about your life before you became a Christian (or before you learned about who Jesus is). You do not need to give intimate details, but focus on the events or feelings that have compelled you to search for the truth.

_____

_____

_____

2. Write how you came to a faith relationship with Christ. At what point did you realize that Jesus was the primary focus of your life?

_____

_____

_____

3. Describe how God has changed you and what God is doing in your life today. If you are not yet a Christian, share how learning about Christ has impacted you personally and the roadblocks you think may be keeping you from deciding to become a Christian now.

_____

_____

_____

Part 3
Living in Faith and Service

9

SESSION NINE
SPIRITUAL DISCIPLINES:
KEYS TO GOD'S HEART

Prepare for the Session

Supplies Needed
- chalkboard or dry-erase board and markers
- Bibles
- participant books
- pens/pencils

Contact the people you enlisted for your panel discussion and make sure they have all the information they need to discuss their assigned spiritual discipline(s) and the impact of that discipline on their lives. Remind them to emphasize their personal experience with the spiritual discipline—their personal struggles and successes—rather than listing "how-to's."

The Importance of Keys

After an opening prayer and welcome, ask group members to call out which key in their possession they cannot live without. Why is that? Ask, "Have you ever lost your keys? What happened?" After two or three people have had the opportunity to share their experiences, tell the group that in this session we will explore keys God has given us to help us in our spiritual journey. We may not think about keys often and may take them for granted but they are clearly important for us to have in order to get where we need to go and do what we need to do each day. Through the Bible, God teaches us about specific "keys" (spiritual disciplines) that we need to have and use in order to get where we need to go and do what we need to do spiritually. These are "keys" to God's heart that open up an intimate relationship with our Creator.

These keys are called spiritual disciplines because they are life practices that come by choice in our lives. Webster's *New World Dictionary* defines discipline as "training that develops self-control" (Second College Edition [Simon and Schuster, 1982]; p. 401). Internal discipline gives us the ability to choose God's way. It involves a series of choices we make over and over to allow God to control our nature and develop our best selves, becoming a new creation in God's image. Using these disciplines is something we decide to do and work at; it doesn't happen automatically. In fact, spiritual disciplines are not generally what we do naturally or easily; but once we choose to incorporate them into our lives on a regular and consistent basis, they become rewarding habits that produce a "harvest of righteousness and peace" in us (Hebrews 12:10-11). They become agents of transformation in our lives.

Defining Spiritual Disciplines

Have the class divide into groups of four to six. They are to read Hebrews 12:10-11 and discuss together the following questions on discipline:

- According to these verses, what positive results will you experience in your life as a result of discipline?
- Why do you think God didn't make spiritual growth automatic?
- As an adult, are you now glad that your parents did or did not discipline you? Why or why not?
- What does your response say about the value of discipline in personal or spiritual growth?

Write the following list of spiritual disciplines on the board and briefly explain each one as you go through the list.

The classic spiritual disciplines include Bible study, prayer, meditation, worship, simplicity, giving, fasting, witnessing, journaling, solitude, submission, service, confession, and guidance. Using these disciplines is much more than going through an activity as part of a daily "to-do" list. The disciplines are not an end in themselves or a way to earn favor with God. They are tools that help us seek God, get to know Jesus better, and to live life as he taught. Through their use we hear God and are able to discern our life path. As we keep using these tools, we allow the Holy Spirit to change and refine us into Christ's image and we will become the person God had in mind even before we were born. We will grow in relationship with our Creator and experience the peace that only connection with that Creator can bring.

> The classic spiritual disciplines include:
>
> Bible study
> prayer
> meditation
> worship
> simplicity
> giving
> fasting
> witnessing
> journaling
> solitude
> submission
> service
> confession
> guidance

Introduce the panelists who have come to share with the group and share which spiritual discipline(s) each will talk about. Allow five to six minutes for each presentation. Invite them to begin and encourage participants to ask questions of the panelists after their talks.

Group Discussion

Following the panel discussion, have participants return to their small groups. Have them discuss the "Biblical Lifestyle of Generosity" from pages 83–84 in the participant book (Leader Guide, pp. 100–01) using the following questions:

- What speaks to you from this statement on giving?
- What do you believe are the biggest challenges in giving according to biblical standards, and what are the best ways to overcome those challenges?

Reflection

Have each participant quietly evaluate their own personal spiritual practices and identify ways the ideas presented by the panel challenge or encourage them. Have them answer using the following questions:

- Which disciplines that you are not currently practicing do you think God wants to use to transform your life?
- When will you begin practicing this discipline?

Seeking God With All Your Heart

As a closing, invite a participant to read Jeremiah 29:13 aloud:

"When you search for me, you will find me;
if you seek me with all your heart."

We will find God if we seek God wholeheartedly. We may passionately want to know God personally; but we need a focus for that passion, a way to direct it, hone it, and point it toward God's heart. The spiritual disciplines give us the focus and direction our passion needs to help us know God. Followers of Jesus have used them as instruments for personal spiritual growth for thousands of years. As we discipline ourselves to consistently use these tools, we open ourselves to the Holy Spirit to change and refine us.

Closing Prayer

Thank you, God, for giving us spiritual disciplines that draw us into your presence and help us build intimacy with you every day. Help me strengthen my resolve to practice these disciplines and to trust that you will meet with me as I do.

Homework

Ask participants to read and complete Session Ten in the participant book. If you are using *Spiritual Entrepreneurs* as an additional resource, also assign Chapter 4, "The Covenant Principle," to read before the next session.

Biblical Lifestyle of Generosity

Throughout the Scriptures, God emphasizes that people who follow God are to also reflect the nature of God. An overpowering characteristic of God is generosity. We are taught to give as God gives to us. As the Holy Spirit lives in us, our lives reflect God's lifestyle of generosity.

In the Old Testament, God, the Creator and Owner of everything, was very clear in expecting us to reciprocate in the giving process. As God freely gives to us, that same attitude is expected in return.

A term introduced in the Old Testament is *tithe*. The Law required the giving of tithes, or one-tenth of a person's gross income, to God. This was seen as a mandatory gift that supported the leaders and activities of God's ministry. However, the people were assured that in spite of required giving, God would meet their daily needs.

As the story unfolds, three responses to God's mandate to give emerged. Some of God's people became casualties of a common struggle—greed. In order to have more for themselves, they stopped giving their ten percent. The second response involved people who continued to give, but out of duty and obligation, not out of love for God. Thirdly, there was always the faithful core who continued in giving as God directed.

As we move into the New Testament, we sense a shift in the emphasis on the amount to give. New covenant believers, recognizing that they are under the Lordship (ownership) of God, see all of their income as belonging to God—not just the tithe. In fact, the New Testament understanding is that Christians are to keep only what they need to provide for themselves and their families. While freely giving, they are not to become a drain on the resources of others. So we must ask ourselves, "What is a reasonable amount required to meet my family's current and future needs?" The amount beyond this is what is given to promote God's work.

The New Testament takes the Old Testament standard to a new level: generosity. This explains the minimal amount of direct teaching in the New Testament on the subject of tithing. According to the New Testament, tithing is only the beginning of giving. For Christians whose income is limited and barely meets their needs, tithing is a goal to achieve. For wealthier Christians, whose income exceeds their needs, the tithe becomes restrictive. We are to go beyond tithing in proportion to how God gives to us. We are to be channels for the resources of God to flow through, not dams holding back God's goodness for ourselves.

It is appropriate for a local church to expect their members to contribute at least a tenth of their income to that local church. This enables the local church to operate as God intended, and both Old and New Testaments support such a stand. Beyond the tithe giving becomes gifts and offerings for God's work.

10

SESSION TEN

THE CHURCH: COMMUNITY OF CHRIST

Prepare for the Session

Supplies Needed
- chalkboard or dry-erase board and markers
- Bibles
- participant books
- If this class is your church's pathway to membership, provide copies of the "Membership Interview Form" or forms provided by your church.
- large pieces of newsprint and markers in a variety of colors
- pens/pencils

More information on the "what" and "why" of the church is available to you on the Ginghamsburg UMC website (http://ginghamsburg.org). The sermons from Michael Slaughter titled "Why the Church" and "Why Methodist" provide helpful background for talking with participants about the content of this lesson.

Membership Pathway

If you are using this class as the membership pathway for your local church, we have included a membership interview form (pp. 111–14) to use with each prospective member. At Ginghamsburg Church, once this class is completed, we provide a one-on-one meeting between the prospective member and a church representative to go over their commitment to the responsibilities of membership, to assist them in finding a small group for growth and accountability, and to help them find their place of ministry. This personal touch for each person reassures them of the church's investment in their growth and empowers them to serve. Other ideas on using this as a membership class can be found on pages 6–7 of this Leader Guide.

Ice Breaker

After greeting the group with a welcome and a prayer, share that today's session will be a time of thinking and learning about the church and its role and purpose here on earth.

Ask the group to divide into groups of four to six. Have each group member jot down their responses to the following three things then discuss them with their group:

- Your first memory of "church"
- What you feel the main role of the church is
- What has been most meaningful to you about your church connection

What Is the Purpose of the Church?

Call the groups back together and ask each to share a couple of things from their discussions. Ask a class member to read the following excerpt from Dr. Paul Brand and Philip Yancey as the rest of the class follows along in their participant books.

Jesus, the exact likeness of God in flesh, expressed the image of God in human form. But from the very beginning He warned that His physical presence was temporary. He had in mind a further goal: to restore the broken image of God in humanity.

God's activity on earth did not end with Jesus, and His image on earth did not vanish when Jesus departed. New Testament authors extend the term to a new Body God is creating composed of "members"—men and women joining together to do the work of God. In referring to this Body, these writers pointedly used the same word that first described the spark of the divine in man and later described Christ. We are called, said Paul, to be "the likeness [image] of his Son, that he might be the firstborn among many brothers" (Romans 8:29b). (Zondervan, 1984; pp. 39–40)

Ask the group how their original perception of the church compares to the idea of our purpose presented in this excerpt.

The church consists of the men and women who have chosen to follow Jesus joining together to do the work of God. When Jesus left the earth, he left his mission in our hands. There is no "Plan B." We are God's representatives on earth, called to help restore the broken image of God in humanity.

The church is more than an organization or structure. It is an organism that is made up of living parts—a living representation of Christ on earth. It is not a perfect representation by any means because it is filled with imperfect people like you and me. In 2 Corinthians 4:6-7, the apostle Paul described humans as "jars of clay"—frail and fallible human beings. It is through just such "broken vessels" that God chooses to be revealed to the world. It is through such "broken vessels" that God releases the power to bring about God's desired outcome for the world.

Group Discussion

Have participants return to their groups, and give each group a large sheet of newsprint and markers in different colors. Assign each of the groups one of the following groups of Scriptures—either those describing "what" the church is or those describing the

"why" or "purpose" of the church. These Scriptures are also found in the participant book (pp. 87, 89).

Say to the class, "Your goal as a group is to create a mural that answers the questions you have been assigned: either *What is the church?* or *What is the purpose of the church?* Use the Scriptures provided to answer your question, then work together to create a visual representation of the answer. The mural can include symbols, words, or pictures. Don't worry about the quality of your 'art.' The goal is to communicate your answer visually, not win an award for your drawing talent!" **Encourage every group member to participate in some fashion by reading Scripture aloud, offering opinions, suggesting ideas, or drawing a portion of the mural.**

What Is the Church?

Acts 2:44-47	*A community of believers*
Romans 12:4-5	*A community of believers*
1 Corinthians 12:12-14, 27	*A unified people*
1 Corinthians 12:21-25	*The body of Christ*
2 Corinthians 6:18	*God's family*
Ephesians 2:19-20	*God's family*
Ephesians 4:3-6	*A unified people*
Revelation 19:6-8	*The bride of Christ*
Revelation 21:1-3	*The bride of Christ*

What Is the Purpose of the Church?

John 13:34-35	*Demonstrate love*
1 Corinthians 10:31	*Glorify God*
2 Corinthians 4:5	*Preach the Word*
Galatians 6:9-10	*Do good works*
Ephesians 2:10	*Do good works*
Ephesians 3:20-21	*Glorify God*
Ephesians 4:11-12	*Equip the saints*
2 Timothy 4:1-2	*Preach the Word*
Hebrews 10:24-25	*Mutual encouragement*

When the groups finish their murals, have them take turns sharing their "art" with the larger group. As they do so, tape the murals to a wall so they are displayed through the rest of class. Be sure to congratulate groups on their insight and creativity.

What Is the Church Meant to Be?

In the Bible, God uses the metaphor of the body to help us understand the interconnectedness of his followers on earth. Just like the human body, the spiritual body of Christ is made up of living, breathing parts, all controlled by the head (Jesus). Each follower of Jesus is a part of the body, intimately connected to and needed by the other parts. Each of us receives instructions from the head, lives under Jesus' authority and control, and passes those instructions on to the parts of the body connected to us.

It is interesting to note the terms used in Scripture to describe the connection between God and God's followers, as well as the connection between individual followers of Jesus. The Bible uses words like *body, bride, family,* and *community.* Each of those terms describes a group of people bound together by commitment, deep care, and common interests, beliefs, and values. Marriage, family, and community are covenantal relationships, meaning they are relationships based on covenants, vows, and promises. Participants in those relationships are called to long-term commitment, living together for better or worse by demonstrating the faithfulness of God to each other. Obviously God takes our connection with God and with other followers seriously.

Scripture also consistently uses the term *unity* to describe these relationships. While each of us is created to be unique and to have a unique place within the body, God expects harmony among us. In other words, God wants a unified body, but doesn't require uniformity. We celebrate individual differences and the joy of diversity. There are areas that we can agree to disagree, but we need to be united on the basic tenets of the faith.

The Church's Purpose

Since Jesus is no longer here in human form, we are the only hands and feet he has on earth. We are God's distribution system. We are to continue Jesus' mission, in the power of the Spirit, by demonstrating love, spreading his word, serving, equipping the saints for ministry, and above all, glorifying and honoring God. Together, through our combined gifts, we touch the world for Jesus.

In order for the church to fulfill its role in the world, we must each personally discover and fulfill our roles in the church, both locally and globally. Every church though organic in nature, needs to be organized to help each person find his or her place to serve within the body of Christ. We need to remember that any organization or structure is there to support the living purpose and mission of the church, not the other way around. The structure must be flexible and fluid enough to change as the needs and ministry approach of the church change.

Discussion

Do a brief presentation that explains the organizational structure of your local church. Be sure to include information regarding the role of the pastor, the pastoral staff, small groups, the mission of the church, and any other information your participants may find relevant to understanding how your church is organized. Or, a couple of weeks ahead of this session ask a member of your pastoral team or other church leader to join you for this session so that he or she can make the presentation and answer any questions your participants may have. It is appropriate at this point to review your church's membership expectations.

This is an appropriate place to include the discussion of Chapter 4 of *Spiritual Entrepreneurs* if you are using this resource. Ask the class the following discussion questions:

- How do the membership requirements of your church compare to what John Wesley required of his followers?
- What does it mean to be a body life member?
- What implications does this have for church membership today?

Conclusion

The church is not a building where people go but God's people in community doing what God has called us to do. The church is a living organism that brings change to the people of the world. We know Christ through worship, study, prayer, submission, and obedience. We make Christ known to others through loving, teaching, serving, and sharing our faith. Both are accomplished through our connection with the church.

There is a place reserved for you within this organism called the body of Christ, including a specific purpose to serve for the benefit of others. It is important that we each discover God's unique call on our lives. In Session Eleven we will investigate how to go about discovering God's call for each of us.

Reflection

Take a few minutes to prayerfully assess what God's call might be for you within the body of Christ. Where do you think God wants you to serve others within Christ's body?

Closing Prayer

I praise you, God, for allowing me to be a part of the body and mission of God here on earth. Thank you for the church family where we each find inspiration and support for our part of God's mission. Guide me in how and where you want me to serve.

Homework

Homework

11

If any participants are considering committing to membership at your local church, give them a membership interview form (see pp. 111–14) and ask them to complete it and bring it to their one-on-one conference with one of the church leaders. This form becomes the basis of discussion for their time with a church leader before membership weekend. It is an affirmation of who the prospective member is and his or her commitment to the church. It is also a place to indicate where they feel called to serve within the church body and be helped in making that connection. Make sure there will be an opportunity for participants to sign up for a conference time after class today.

Ask students to read and complete Session Eleven in the participant book. If you are using *Spiritual Entrepreneurs* as an additional resource, also assign Chapter 5, "The Priesthood Principle," to read before the next session.

Membership Interview Form

The following is a statement of my faith and my commitment to the body of Christ as I seek to enter membership at my local church.

Name_____Birthdate_____
Address_____
_____

Home Phone_____Work Phone_____
Cell Phone_____Email address_____

My Story

Please write below in your own words how you came to know Jesus Christ as Lord and savior.

_____
_____
_____
_____
_____
_____
_____
_____
_____
_____
_____
_____
_____
_____
_____
_____
_____
_____

Who influenced you to first visit our church?
Name_____

Requirements to Become a Member

1. I've accepted Jesus Christ into my life and know him personally as my savior and Lord. (Please check the most appropriate statement for you.) Before coming to this church, I was:

   __a pre-Christian without active church involvement.

   __a Christian but not actively attending a church.

   __attending a church but not a Christian.

   __a Christian and active member/participant in church.

2. I have been baptized.

   __yes, when?_____

   __planning on it before membership weekend

   __let's talk

3. I've completed (or will complete) all my *Following Jesus* homework or make-up work including my membership interview appointment:

   __yes

   __will soon (by _____)

   __let's talk

Responsibilities of Membership

1. I will regularly attend a weekly worship celebration.

   __yes

   __not really

   __let's talk

2. I will seek regular involvement in a cell group for discipleship, nurture, and accountability.

   __yes

   __not really

   __let's talk

   __already in a group, the leaders are: _____

3. I am committed to consistent tithing to my local church's ministry and to go beyond as God leads.
   __yes
   __not really
   __let's talk

4. I will take advantage of adult education classes for continued learning and discipleship.
   __yes
   __not really
   __let's talk

5. I will, upon completion of my membership interview appointment, strive to consistently use my spiritual gifts as I minister to others.
   __yes
   __not really
   __let's talk

After taking the spiritual gifts inventory, in which three gift areas did you score highest?

Gift	Score
a. _____	_____
b. _____	_____
c. _____	_____

What have you identified as your ministry passion?

_____

_____

_____

Circle your ministry interaction style:
   Quadrant 1- People   Quadrant 2- Task
   Quadrant 3- Lead, Organize, Plan Quadrant 4- Support, Behind
                                         the Scenes

Based upon your spiritual giftedness, ministry passion, and ministry interaction style, please list any ministry(ies) in which you're currently involved or in which you would like to serve. Keep in mind our challenge to you to commit to a primary ministry and serve fully there.

_____

_____

_____

How would you describe your practice of personal spiritual disciplines? (Bible study, prayer, giving, meditation, journaling, fasting, etc.)

_____

_____

_____

Describe how you are growing as a follower of Jesus. How is your life changing as a result of being in relationship with Jesus?

_____

_____

_____

I understand the requirements and responsibilities of membership listed above. I hereby commit myself to the Lord Jesus and his body—the church. I will strive to live out my membership commitments in a way that honors Christ so his kingdom is advanced.

Signature_____

Date_____

11

SESSION ELEVEN
UNDERSTANDING GOD'S CALL

Prepare for the Session

Supplies Needed
- chalkboard or dry-erase board and markers
- Bibles
- participant books
- pens/pencils

After an opening prayer and welcome, share with the group that we are all on life's great unfolding adventure—discovering God's call on our lives. Although many of us say that we chose Jesus, the reality is that Jesus first chose us (John 15:16). Jesus chose us to be about his business, which is reaching out to those who do not yet know him and joining with others to serve in his name.

If you are using *Spiritual Entrepreneurs* as a resource, lead the class in a discussion of Chapter 5, "The Priesthood Principle." Ask the following questions:

- What is the priesthood principle?
- How do ordinary people dream God's dream?
- What are you dreaming?

Sometimes we may think that the pastor and church staff—the "paid professionals"—are the ones called by God to do God's work. A look at the New Testament church of the first century gives insight into how God's church is to operate. Look at Acts 8:1-4, which took place following the martyrdom of Stephen:

> On that day a great persecution broke out against the church in Jerusalem, and all except the apostles were scattered throughout Judea and Samaria. Godly men buried Stephen and mourned deeply for him. But Saul began to destroy the church. Going from house to house, he dragged off both men and women and put them in prison. Those who had been scattered preached the word wherever they went.

As the result of persecution, the early church spread throughout the known world. There was not an expectation of the apostles doing all the work. In fact, it was the ordinary people, who had been forced out of Jerusalem, who were preaching the Word wherever they went. There was no longer a separation between the priesthood and ordinary followers as there had been in the Old Testament system. The understanding in the new covenant is that all Christ's followers function as priests: representing people to God and representing God to people. Each follower has been given a custom-designed way of doing that by God.

To discover God's call on our lives, we have to take time to look inward and ask ourselves some meaningful questions about our passions and our desires, as well as our gifts and abilities. In this session, you will go on a private, inward journey.

Group Discussion

Divide participants into groups of four or six and ask them to read through Acts 8:1-4 again and answer the following questions:
- How was the church dispersed from Jerusalem to Judea and Samaria? What did those scattered do?
- What is the significance of ordinary people being given responsibility for fulfilling God's mission on earth?
- What are different ways that the Word can be "preached"? Which way do you feel God has equipped you to share the good news about Jesus?

Discovering God's Call

Read Psalm 139:13-16.

There is a plan for each one of us that is specifically designed by God and prepared for us before time began. This is what we refer to as our call from God. Each of us in our Christian walk must answer the questions: *What is my call?* and *How do I personally carry out the ministry of Jesus?*

Group Discussion

To proceed with this quest, it helps to follow a plan that leads us in discovering what God has created us to do. This plan is repeatable; you can go through the steps of this plan each time you are trying to discern the next step in God's call for you. **Ask participants to turn to pages 93–96 in the participant book to follow along with this plan. As class members read the Scriptures, write on the chalkboard or dry-erase board the steps to discovering God's call.**

Step 1

The first step in discovering God's call on your life is to surrender yourself to God.
Read Matthew 16:24-25 and Romans 12:1-2.

We must surrender everything to Jesus. Surrender is not easy for any of us. We are taught to be independent, self-sufficient, make-your-own-decision kind of people. But to allow Jesus to be Lord, we must surrender ourselves to him and give him permission to carry out his plan through us.

Take a few moments to identify if there is any area of your life that you have yet to surrender to God. As you identify areas, silently give each one to God.

Step

2

The second step is to listen to God.
Read Jeremiah 29:11-13 and Deuteronomy 30:19-20.
Through the Word of God, we learn that our Creator has a plan for each of us. God will tell us what that plan is and guide us step by step if we take time to listen. Even though we know God is loving and just, we may be fearful of what we will hear or what God may ask us to do. This fear is unnecessary, because God's will for our lives is born out of God's love for us. We must lay aside our reservations, be willing to risk, and listen to God. Only by listening can we discern God's call for our lives.

Take some time now and listen to God in silence. As you listen, write down anything you hear the Holy Spirit saying to you. Be sensitive to the thoughts and internal nudges that may be God speaking to you. Throughout life, you will hear God in many ways—through God's Word, through silent prayer like you are practicing now, or through the voices of other people speaking to you. The assurance is that over time you will learn to recognize God's voice and train yourself to respond in obedience.

Give participants a moment or two to sit quietly and write in their participant books.

Step

3

The third step is to confirm who is speaking.
Once you believe you have heard from God, the next step is to test what you have heard. Not everything we think we hear really comes from God. There are many other voices within us competing for attention. Our own desires, fears, understanding, and the voice of the enemy all battle for dominance in our attempts to hear God in our spirits.

Below are some of the questions you must ask yourself to determine whether the call you hear is really from God or from some other source. If you cannot answer yes to all these questions, then you may need to rethink whether the call you have heard is really from God.

Is it scriptural? Is the call you are considering consistent with the commands and principles of God's Word? God will never call you to do anything that goes against what is taught in Scripture.

Does it glorify Christ? The purpose of following God's call is not to glorify or call attention to us, but to point others to Jesus and life in him. Anything that glorifies a person above God or dishonors Christ is not of God.

Is it my passion? God created each of us to be unique. Each of us has different things that bring us joy. God's plan for us is designed to fit the way we are made. As a result, we often have a strong desire to serve in a way that fits with the deepest desires of our hearts.

Is it consistent with my gifts and talents? If we are searching for the way God will use us, it only makes sense that God's plan for us would match up with and use the spiritual gifts and talents God has given us. What talents and gifts has God given you? Do these match up with the call you are considering?

Does it meet a need? As you look around the community where you live, can you see how this call can genuinely help other people? God does not call us to do things that are purely self-focused. Anything God calls us to do has the ultimate goal of serving others, meeting their needs, and helping them to know God.

What is the counsel of other believers? Those believers who know you well can give you wise counsel as you attempt to discover God's will for you. Being a part of a small group where you are prayed for, encouraged, and held accountable will develop friends who can give you honest feedback and share with you what you may not be able to see for yourself.

Have each participant focus on what God call they may be hearing or on a decision they need to make. Take a few moments to assess what you believe God may be saying to you about God's call for you. Answer each of the above questions with that in mind.

Step

The fourth step is trusting God.

Following God can seem risky because we give up control over our own destinies. Where will God take us? What will God call us to do? Will God protect us and keep us from making mistakes?

Read Deuteronomy 7:9; 1 Corinthians 1:4-9; and Psalm 22:5.

God is not safe in the human sense of the word. The Bible makes it clear that God can and will allow God's children to make mistakes and to suffer. But God is good and intends the best possible outcome for us. And that is why we can trust God, wherever God leads. When we step out in faith, God will not disappoint us. We can depend on God to be faithful in keeping God's promises.

Reflection

Take the next moments to prayerfully answer the following questions:

- What did you learn about yourself during your study of this session?
- What did you learn about discovering God's call on your life?
- What's one way you think God has called you to serve?

We have talked about unique, personal calls from God on the lives of God's followers. But there are some things all Christians are called to do such as loving one another, supporting God's mission with our tithes and gifts, sharing our faith, and pursuing a Christ-like lifestyle. Even as you are exploring what specific call God has placed on your life, you can serve God by obediently doing those things.

Closing Prayer

Write a brief prayer to God, telling how you feel about the call God has placed on your life. Tell God how you feel about letting go of your own plans in favor of God's plans for you. Ask God to strengthen your faith so that you can follow God's will boldly, with all your heart. Thank God for choosing you and for the unique call God has placed on your life. Let God know that you trust God to reveal your call to you a step at a time.

Homework

Ask students to read and complete Session Twelve. If you are using *Spiritual Entrepreneurs* as an additional resource, also assign Chapter 6, "The Leadership Principle," to read before the next session.

Homework 12

12

SESSION TWELVE
GOD'S PLACE FOR YOU

Prepare for the Session

Supplies Needed
- chalkboard or dry-erase board and markers
- Bibles
- participant books
- pens/pencils

The final session of this class is both celebratory and insightful. Share with the class that the intersection of their gifts, passion, and personality is the unique God-given place of service for each person. Today we will look at that for each participant and help launch each one into meaningful ministry.

If you are using *Spiritual Entrepreneurs* as an additional resource, following an opening prayer, begin the class with a discussion of Chapter 6, "The Leadership Principle." Ask the following questions:

- What is the difference between a leader and a manager?
- What are the key functions of a leader? To which function do you most relate?
- In which situations or relationships do you serve as a leader (your job, your ministry, as a parent, etc.)? How has this chapter helped you sharpen your leadership abilities?

Icebreaker

Have participants share in small groups an excuse they have used to avoid doing something they did not want to do. After a few minutes, call everyone together and have participants share some of the answers from their groups.

Once several persons have shared, say: "Can you think of a time recently when you used an excuse to avoid doing something? We all use silly excuses at times to get out of doing things. Sometimes we even use excuses to avoid things we really want to do but are afraid to try. We may be afraid of failure (or success), or perhaps we're afraid we will make the wrong choice. That's how it often is for Christians when they first step out to serve in the church. Deep down they may really want to serve; but they are afraid, so they make excuses.

"If that has been your experience, don't worry. You are in good company! Even Moses, one of the greatest followers of God in the Bible, made excuses when God called him at the burning bush. Let's look at some of the excuses Moses made. I suspect that at least some of them will look familiar."

Have someone in each small group read Exodus 3:1-10. Allow a few moments for each person to individually answer the questions in their participant books and discuss them briefly at their table:

- Describe how and to what God is calling Moses.
- In what ways have you heard God's call?

Say to the class, "This was Moses' call from God. Delivering Israel from Egypt was exactly what Moses had been created to do. His personality, his gifts, his upbringing, and his life experiences all made him the perfect man for the job. But Moses was afraid, and he made excuses. Let's look at some of the excuses he made."

Have each small group read the Scripture passages from Exodus (also listed on p. 100 of the participant book) and find the excuses Moses used to avoid doing what God was calling him to do.

When the groups have finished their assignment, call the class together and discuss their answers to the questions. Include the following information in your discussion as needed:

Exodus 3:11-12—Who am I? Moses reflected his deep-seated sense of unworthiness to be used by God. God countered by reminding Moses that serving and obedience are about God's sufficiency, not Moses' ability. All God asked of Moses was his availability; God would fill in the rest. We need to remember God's promise to Moses as we use the excuse of unworthiness.

Exodus 3:13-15—Moses was slow to acknowledge who was behind this call to serve and feared others would not recognize God either. Moses was basically asking, "Who are you to be sending me? Why should I go when others will question what I am doing?" God put the power and recognition of the name of God behind Moses. God will do the same with us in our area of service.

Exodus 4:1-9—The depth of Moses' insecurity is uncovered in this verse. He feared other people challenging him—"The Lord didn't really appear to you. C'mon, Moses! That just isn't possible!" When we are overly concerned with what other people think, we cave in to peer pressure and follow the crowd rather than God. Like Moses, our job is to obey and follow through with God's call. It is God's job to convince others.

Exodus 4:10-12—Moses shifted to an emphasis on his physical weakness when he realized that God was not buying into any of his excuses so far. Now Moses reminded God, "I am slow of speech and tongue." (Many biblical scholars think Moses may have experienced stuttering.) God responded, again, by telling Moses that God is not concerned with Moses' abilities but his availability. In 2 Corinthians 12:9-10 we see this same principle: God's power is made perfect through our weaknesses. People see our weakness, and our ability to serve God effectively tells them it's not about us but God working through us.

Exodus 4:13-17—Moses used up all his excuses and resorted to pleading with God to "please send someone else." Moses simply didn't want to do what God asked. Because we don't feel like it, it's inconvenient, or we're afraid, our tendency is to push our responsibility to obey God's call off on someone else. And God's response, as with Moses, is anger. God wants to use us, not just because it furthers God's plan, but because we are wired to give and serve. We will never grow into our full potential until we respond to and obey God's call. God will make God's plan happen, through us or someone else. When God moves on to someone else, the loss is ours. God, as a loving father, however, continues to give us chances to serve God. Even if we have made excuses and missed opportunities in the past, our future opens up with so much potential as we decide to respond to God affirmatively now.

Group Discussion

Ask participants:
- Are any of these excuses familiar?
- What are modern-day equivalent excuses that Christians use?
- How can you, like Moses, overcome your excuses in order for God to use you?

Using Your Call

In Session Eleven, we walked through the steps involved in discovering the call God has placed upon each one of us. Today we'll go one step further to come to an understanding of where to use that call within the church and our local community. To do that, follow the directions in these three areas, then discuss your answers with the others in your group. **(Direct participants to pages 101–02 in the participant book.)**

Your Passions

To discover your passions, write down your answers to the following questions:

- If you had no restrictions on your time or money, what kinds of people or special causes would you like to help?
- What group of people or special cause would you like to serve in order to leave a legacy or make a difference?
- What would your spouse or closest friend say you are passionate about?

Your Spiritual Gifts

Think about the spiritual gifts God has given you. Go back and review Session Seven about spiritual gifts. Write down your spiritual gifts that you identified from that session.

Your Personality Style

To help identify your personality style, or how God has wired you, write down your answers to the following questions:

- Do you prefer to work with people or do you prefer to work on a task without interacting with people very much?
- Do you prefer doing things that require you to lead, plan, and organize events or people or do you prefer to work in a supporting role behind the scenes?

Now, to find your place in the local church and community, pull the information from these three areas together. Is there a kind of service in which all of these areas intersect? Think about ways of serving your church and community that will use your passions, spiritual gifts, and personality style. Write down your ideas and discuss them with your study leader.

Reflection

Everything we have studied in the last twelve sessions can be summed up in the word *discipleship*. We have discovered God's expectations of God's children. It is now up to you to take this information and let it, in the power of the Holy Spirit, transform your life.

Closing Prayer

Lord, thank you for your presence and your movement in my life through this study. I praise you for daily opportunities to be transformed into Christ's image. I pray for the leaders and other participants in this study as they too take the next step in discipleship and service to God. Thank you for their influence on my spiritual growth.

Continuing Work

Work with your church leader to find a place of service and a small group of other believers for accountability and encouragement. Then serve and live passionately and wholeheartedly.

Ask participants to complete the Evaluation (participant book, p. 104; Leader Guide, p. 127) before leaving class today. Collect these when finished.

Evaluation

We are so glad that you have been part of this study. Your presence has helped encourage all of us! We celebrate how far we've come together. It would be helpful to us to hear your thoughts on your experience in this class. Please answer these last three questions:

1. What has been especially meaningful to you in the past twelve sessions?

_____

_____

_____

2. Which sessions have you taken to heart and already implemented in your life?

_____

_____

_____

3. What is the next step in your discipleship process?

_____

_____

_____

When you are finished, please leave your answers with your study leader.

Made in the USA
Middletown, DE
30 January 2020